Years of DESPAIR
1929-1939

Michiel Horn

Grolier Limited
TORONTO

CENTURY OF CANADA SERIES

SERIES CONSULTANT: DESMOND MORTON

Dedicated to Cornelia.

Illustration credits: Public Archives of Canada, pages 6 (C29461), 22 (C9064), 25 (C27900), 28 (C29397), 34 (top left C47404, top right C20013, bottom PA35133), 54 (PA52600), 59, 61, 62 (C21562), 65 (C68509), 67 (C19516), 73 (C27901), 76 (C30811), 82, 92 (C2178), 99 (C67451), 103 (PA119013); Metro Toronto Library Board, pages 14, 74; Saskatchewan Archives Board, pages 8, 9, 36, 51; Manitoba Archives, page 18; Glenbow Archives, pages 31, 41, 44, 63; Vancouver Public Library, page 37; Provincial Archives of Alberta, page 47; Ontario Archives, page 64. Page 88, clockwise from top left: Ontario Archives, Public Archives of Canada C30804, C29492, Air Canada, Ontario Archives, Callander Museum.

Canadian Cataloguing in Publication Data

Horn, Michiel, 1939–
  Years of despair, 1929–1939

(Century of Canada series)
Includes index.
ISBN 0-7172-1861-9

1. Depressions—1929—Canada.   2. Canada—History—1918–1939. *
3. Canada—Economic conditions—1918–1945. *   4. Canada—Social conditions—1930–1939. *   I. Title.   II. Series.

FC577.H67 1986   971.062'3   C86-094284-8

1234567890   THB   09876

Printed and Bound in Canada

CONTENTS

FOREWORD

There was nothing new about depressions in Canada. Most people alive in the 1930s had lived through two bad ones—in 1913-14 and in 1920-22. The Great Depression of the 1930s spread despair because it lasted so long, because it was accompanied by a man-made ecological disaster on the prairies and because nothing, short of a Second World War, seemed to make any difference.

Some influential Canadians helped spread despair during the Depression. They claimed that there were plenty of jobs if people would only look for them. They insisted that the crisis was due to a "minor correction" in an otherwise perfect system. They explained that widespread misery fell on people who had not "saved for a rainy day." A few preachers even explained that the Depression was punishment for loose morals, short skirts and high living during the twenties.

Yet we know now that these were also years when ideas were shaped that could save Canada from future economic catastrophes. Out of the thirties, Canadians learned how to manage their economy. They got a Bank of Canada, federal unemployment insurance and the basis for a much fairer sharing of national wealth among provinces and people. They also learned that high tariffs, economic protectionism and other "beggar your neighbour" policies help make economic folly.

Reading about these "Years of Despair" may help us to remember some lessons our own elders seem to have forgotten.

Michiel Horn is probably the leading Canadian historian of the Depression decade. He is a special expert on the economic and social ideas which might have cut short the Depression and which helped prevent its return for almost fifty years. No one is better fitted to lead us through years we may barely recognize from our own age of renewed unemployment, food banks and economic crisis.

Desmond Morton
University of Toronto

EVENTS 1929-39

Year	Canada	The World
1929	— "Persons" decision by the Judicial Committee of the Imperial Privy Council opens Senate doors to women. — Stock and commodity markets crash. — Drought begins in Saskatchewan.	— Herbert Hoover inaugurated as president of U.S. — Prices for grains and other natural products begin to decline. — Stock and commodity markets crash.
1930	— R.B. Bennett's Conservatives win the federal election. — Cairine Wilson becomes first woman appointed to Senate.	— Austria and Italy sign friendship treaty. — Smoot–Hawley Tariff (U.S.) damages Canadian agricultural exports. — Planet Pluto discovered.
1931	— Estevan riot; three strikers killed. — Saskatchewan Relief Commission established. — Tim Buck and seven other Communist leaders jailed.	— British Parliament passes Statute of Westminster defining status of Dominions. — Japan invades Manchuria. — Britain leaves the gold standard.
1932	— Federal government establishes relief camps for transient men. — Canadian Radio Broadcasting Commission formed. — Dominion Drama Festival founded.	— U.S. presidential election: Franklin Delano Roosevelt (Democrat) wins. — Imperial Economic Conference, Ottawa. — Famine in USSR.
1933	— Liberals win provincial elections in British Columbia and Nova Scotia. — Regina Convention of the CCF.	— Nazi leader Adolf Hitler takes office in Germany. — Roosevelt "New Deal" begins in the U.S.
1934	— Newfoundland loses responsible government. — Liberals win provincial elections in Ontario and Saskatchewan. — Action libérale nationale formed. — Dionne quintuplets born.	— German rearmament begins. — World Disarmament Conference breaks up in failure. — Communist International calls for a "united front against fascism."
1935	— R.B. Bennett announces "New Deal." — Federal election: Liberals led by W.L.M. King win. — Provincial election in Alberta: Social Credit victorious. — On-To-Ottawa Trek and Dominion Day Riot in Regina. — Winnipeg Blue Bombers become the first western team to win the Grey Cup. — Bank of Canada established.	— Italy invades Ethiopia. — Congress of Industrial Organizations (CIO) organized in U.S. — First sulfa drug discovered. — First radar equipment built.
1936	— Union Nationale victorious in Quebec provincial election. — Alberta defaults on part of its provincial debt. — Canadian Broadcasting Corporation formed.	— Spanish Civil War begins. — F.D. Roosevelt wins re-election in U.S. — King George V dies; his heir, Edward VIII, abdicates the throne. — Italy completes conquest of Ethiopia.
1937	— Auto workers strike in Oshawa. — Judicial Committee of the Privy Council finds several Bennett "New Deal" Measures to be unconstitutional. — Royal Commission on Dominion–Provincial Relations formed. — Trans-Canada airlines begins service.	— Japan attacks China. — Coronation of King George VI. — Neville Chamberlain becomes prime minister of Britain. — Italy withdraws from League of Nations.
1938	— On-To-Victoria Trek. — National Housing Act passed.	— Czechoslovakian crisis. — Munich agreement.
1939	— King George VI and Queen Elizabeth tour Canada. — Canada declares war on Germany. — Provincial election in Quebec: Liberals defeat Union Nationale.	— Germany and USSR sign non-aggression pact. — Germany invades Poland. — Outbreak of war in Europe, as Britain and France declare war on Germany.

1

A DISMAL DECADE:
SETTING THE STAGE

In Regina, Dominion Day, 1935, began like any other midsummer holiday. By the time it ended it had become a day to remember. An evening meeting in the Market Square turned into a riot. For more than two hours, angry, cursing men used stones, sticks and pieces of scrap metal against policemen's clubs. Then gun shots rang out. A few men sagged to the ground, hit by police bullets, and the rioters gave way and fled. By 10:45, when dusk had settled on the town, the City Commissioner told reporters that the police had restored order. One police detective was dead, however, and more than fifty policemen were hurt. Over fifty rioters and spectators were injured; one of them was in serious condition.

What had gone wrong? Some blamed Communist agitators for the riot; others held the police or the federal government responsible. An official investigation later concluded that the riot had started when people objected to a proper exercise of police duty. Whoever caused the incident, however, it demonstrated two important themes of the Depression years in Canada. One was the frustration of unemployed workers who were unable to earn a living. The other was the determination of the authorities to suppress unwelcome protest.

The July 1 meeting in Regina was one of strikers and their supporters. The former were on strike not against an employer but against the federal government itself. They had been inmates of special Dominion relief camps, set up in 1932 to house, clothe and feed single unemployed men. The camps were mostly in remote places such as northern Ontario and Quebec and the interior of British Columbia. There, supervised by staff of the Department of National Defence, the men worked eight hours a day, six days a week. In exchange they got their meals, a bunk bed in an army hut, work clothes, and a daily allowance of 20 cents which they could spend on tobacco, candy, writing paper, stamps and other small items.

The work was mostly useless. At a few of the camps that were close to cities, the men did work that had some demonstrable value, such as repairing the citadel at Halifax or constructing an airforce base near Ottawa. But most of the projects had no purpose beyond keeping the men occupied and out of the way. They cleared airstrips in the bush for a trans-Canada air service that did not yet exist, or laid out pieces of dirt road leading from nowhere to nowhere. Whenever the projects did have some evident value, employers and construction trade unions in the area usually protested. They argued that it harmed legitimate business and working men's interests to have needed work done by cheap labour.

The inmates became increasingly resentful, conscious that their lives were being wasted in boring work that offered no prospect of anything better. Hostility focussed on the quasi-military discipline in the camps, the lack of privacy and of facilities for

Opposite page: On-to-Ottawa Trek, June 1935. Relief camp strikers reach Regina— and there they will stay, as RCMP prevent all but a small delegation from continuing.

amusement or entertainment, the pointlessness of the work, and the insulting sum of 20 cents a day. That this was described not as a wage but as an allowance seemed to emphasize the dependence of the men who received it. Some of them listened eagerly to organizers for the Communist-led Relief Camp Workers' Union (RCWU). This union never gained formal recognition, and its organizers were expelled from the camps whenever the authorities were able to identify them. The RCWU nevertheless had some success in uniting camp inmates behind its six demands for change. Of these the most important was "that work with wages be provided at a minimum rate of 50 cents an hour for unskilled labour; union rates for all skilled labour. Such work to be on [the] basis of [a] five-day week, six-hour working day, and minimum of 20 days' work per month."

British Columbia was a hotbed of RCWU activity. There were camp strikes in both 1934 and 1935, as men refused to work. In the spring of 1935 more than a thousand strikers left the camps and gathered in Vancouver. They survived on donations from supporters and by pan-handling. In late May the strike leadership decided that the only way to make an impression on Ottawa was to take the strike there.

Thus the "On-to-Ottawa Trek" was born. The trekkers headed east on CPR freight trains, picking up support and numbers along the way. The federal government regarded them as a serious threat. Prime Minister R.B. Bennett and his cabinet feared there would be violence if thousands of young men demonstrated on Parliament Hill. "Riding the freights" was very common in the 1930s—but it *was* illegal. The Royal Canadian Mounted Police were instructed to stop the trekkers, now about two thousand strong, at Regina. They did so on June 14, but an eight-man delegation was allowed to proceed to Ottawa. The rest waited in tents to see what Ottawa might do for them.

The stormy discussion that took place in Ottawa on June 22 quickly degenerated into an exchange of insults. Prime Minister Bennett called trek leader Arthur "Slim" Evans a criminal; Evans told Bennett he was "not fit to be the premier of a Hottentot village." Not surprisingly, no agreement was reached. The delegates had to return to Regina empty-handed, but they were cheered by supporters along the way. Many Canadians had come to believe that the government's "slave camps" should be closed down and real work provided to the inmates.

Convinced that the trek was a Communist plot and that it would collapse if its leaders were jailed, the Bennett government ordered them arrested for criminal sedition. For the police, the key question was when it would be easiest to apprehend them. The answer seemed to lie in a meeting planned for 8:00 P.M. on July 1 in Regina's Market Square. The police knew that Evans and the

ON TO OTTAWA

The Relief Camp Strikers will leave Regina via C.P.R. Freight

Monday, June 17th
at approx. 10 p.m.

The Federal Government have declared an embargo on our leaving Regina by the same means by which we came.

Only the mass support of Regina Citizens will force the Authorities to keep their hands off us on our way to Ottawa.

We call upon every citizen who supports us in our fight against Forced Slave Labor to assemble at the C.P.R. freight yards between Albert and Broad Street

Monday, June 17th from 10 p.m. until we leave

We extend to Regina Citizens our heartiest thanks for their splendid support in this vital issue.

Publicity Committee.
Relief Camp Strikers.

six others for whom they had warrants would probably all be on the platform. They feared, moreover, that the trekkers, frustrated by their enforced stay in Regina, might soon do something desperate. The time therefore seemed ripe. Units of the Regina police, reinforced by the RCMP, moved into the square shortly after 8:00 to make the arrests.

Although they had anticipated the possibility of resistance, the police had not expected the fury with which they were met. They managed to make the arrests, but at the cost of a full-fledged riot. Trekkers and sympathizers both turned on the police. The rage directed itself particularly against the RCMP, whose men had blocked the trekkers for more than two weeks. Sticks, stones, broken car springs and anything else that came to hand soon filled the air, injuring policemen and breaking shop windows along several downtown streets. The police fought back with clubs, charging the crowd in efforts to break it up and force it to disperse. Finally, the police use of firearms brought the riot to an end.

By midnight 120 men were behind bars, Slim Evans among them. Without their leaders, the rank and file of the strikers abandoned the On-to-Ottawa trek and accepted the government's offer to transport them to relief camps. The camps' days were num-

Regina, Dominion Day 1935. A meeting of relief camp strikers and their sympathizers turns into a riot when police try to arrest strike leaders.

bered, however. R.B. Bennett's Conservative government went down to crushing defeat in the election of October 1935. The new Liberal prime minister, William Lyon Mackenzie King, had pledged to close the camps, and he did so in 1936.

Closing the camps did not end unemployment. Many thousands of men roamed the land for the next few years as they had early in the 1930s, hunting for jobs that remained scarce. Not until after the Second World War began in September 1939, did a surplus of workers gradually turn into a shortage. Some of those who rioted in Regina in 1935 did not get their first real job until 1940 or even later. For many Canadians, especially young Canadians, the Depression years were truly years of despair.

Setting the Stage: the Twenties
The Depression of the 1930s has burned its way into Canada's collective memory as "the winter years," "the hungry years," "the dirty thirties." The 1920s, by way of contrast, are remembered as a time of prosperity and excitement. Many people think of those years as "the roaring twenties," an age of jazz, fast cars, "flappers" and "bathtub gin," of sports heroes like baseball's Babe Ruth, and gangsters like Chicago's Al Capone. These images are drawn largely from the United States, indicating the power of the American media. They do not capture the reality of the lives even of most Americans, and they apply still less to Canada. If the 1920s roared, they did so for a minority only. For many Canadians, the twenties were far from being prosperous.

The decade began with a serious economic depression. By 1924 Canada was emerging from this slump, and the next few years witnessed an economic boom that many Canadians came to look back on with nostalgia. In the rosy glow of memory, the twenties came to seem better than, in fact, they were.

Nevertheless, compared to the Depression years that followed them, the later 1920s were a good time economically. A renewed surge of investment in factories, pulp mills, mines, farms, and railway and residential construction brought increased employment and profits. The pattern of investment reflected both optimism about Canada's traditional export industries and a growing emphasis on processing and manufacturing. At the base of much of the expansion of the 1920s was investment in hydro-electricity. This made power available more cheaply than before to mills, mines and factories. Manufacturing was ever more important. The production of automobiles and electrical appliances increased spectacularly. Some of this new production was for export, but Canada continued to rely heavily for export earnings on the products of her fields, forests and mines.

In contrast with most of the raw materials sector, coal mining was depressed throughout the 1920s. This made life very hard for the miners in places like Cape Breton and the Alberta–British Columbia border country. The fisheries, too, were weak, particularly in the Atlantic provinces, a region that did not share in the prosperity of the later 1920s.

On the other hand, prairie agriculture, still centrally important to Canada's economic well-being, enjoyed several strong years. Wheat prices stabilized around $1.45 a bushel, and farmers brought new acreage into production. With the introduction of hardier strains of wheat, yields rose. Favourable weather also helped. In 1928 there was a record crop of 567 million bushels.

A bushel is a unit of dry measure equal to 36.37 litres.

Unemployment was low in the later twenties. Average annual unemployment, which ran at 7 percent in 1925, dropped to 2.9 percent in 1927 and 2.6 percent in 1928. However, many workers earned too little to be able to buy exciting new consumer goods such as radios and refrigerators. Automobiles had long since ceased to be a luxury available only to the very few, but many Canadians could not yet afford a car. In 1929 no more than two in five families had one.

Many Canadians who did have these items had bought them on the installment plan. Consumer credit expanded greatly during the 1920s, particularly for the purchase of automobiles and major appliances.

The average annual earnings of a production worker in 1929 were $1041. The federal Department of Labour estimated that a family needed an annual income of $1200 to $1500, depending on family size, in order to maintain a "minimum standard of decency." Married women and older children often worked outside the home or took in piece-work to raise family income. It is nevertheless likely that at least half of urban Canadians lived at or below the poverty line. They lived in over-crowded dwellings, which were hot in summer and cold in winter, and which often lacked such amenities as baths, toilets and electricity. They suffered from malnutrition, were badly dressed, found it hard to keep themselves and their clothes clean, and suffered from various preventable diseases.

The proportion of the rural population that was poor is harder to guess. Approximately three in ten Canadians still depended directly on agriculture for their livelihood. Some of them prospered; others barely managed to get by. Some depended on other work, such as that provided by logging camps in the winter, to make ends meet. On average, prairie farmers were best off, while those in Quebec and the Atlantic provinces were poorest. Even many well-to-do farmers still lived without electricity and running water, but automobiles were replacing the horse and buggy, particularly on the prairies, and more advanced farm machinery, such as tractors and combines, was coming into wider use.

Yet if a good many farmers did well, farm labourers emphatically did not. Their average annual income in 1929 was $756; that sum included both cash wages and the value of board during the summer season. As miserably poor as farm labourers were, however, they were better off than almost all native people.

	Women as a % of Work Force
1921	15.4
1931	17.0

Most working women were single, widowed or divorced. Very few married women took paid employment unless their incomes were essential to family welfare, either because they had been deserted or because their husbands earned too little.

Who did prosper during the 1920s? Supervisory and office workers did significantly better than other employees, earning an average of $1976 in 1929. This would have made for a reasonably comfortable life, and for a home that was ample in size and well-equipped by the standards of the day, with electrical service and full bathrooms. At this level very few married women worked for pay outside the home. They might well enjoy the part-time assistance of a domestic servant, although labour-saving devices such as vacuum cleaners and washing machines were becoming more common.

Fewer than one in five Canadian families had an annual income of $2000 or more. These families were typically headed by professional and managerial people, businessmen, a handful of skilled workers and farmers, and a small number of the genuinely rich. Only 13 447 Canadian taxpayers, or one in every 300 income earners, reported incomes over $10 000 in 1929. One did not need to earn anywhere close to this much in order to have a full-time live-in servant, normally a young woman and often a recent immigrant, who might earn room, board and perhaps $15 a month for six days of hard work a week.

The evidence of great inequalities of income and wealth troubled few people, and it certainly did not move governments to do anything about them. Important Canadians, including businessmen and politicians, believed that low wages encouraged investment and economic growth. When governments intervened in the economy, it was usually to assist business. Protective tariffs, for example, helped Canadian manufacturers survive and grow. Direct financial aid to industry, however, was less common in the 1920s than it had been before the 1914–18 war. The federal government in particular, burdened with debt as a result of that war, tried to limit its spending. The provincial governments were readier to help business, both directly, in the form of cash grants to enterprises such as railways, and indirectly, as in the construction of highways.

Social services as yet attracted little government interest or money. By and large, people were expected to fend for themselves, and to turn to private charity if they could not. In 1927 Ottawa offered to share the costs of a very limited scheme of old age pensions with any provincial government that cared to introduce it; not all provinces had done so by 1929. Family allowances did not exist, nor did unemployment insurance or public medical care and hospital insurance. Illness was a constant menace to the well-being of many families.

The belief that the 1920s were years of general prosperity is wrong. They were years more prosperous than Canadians would know again for more than a decade, but they saw perhaps a majority of Canadians living in poverty. Furthermore, they contained the seeds of decline. The rate of economic growth was slowing in the twenties, and was lower than it had been before the 1914–18 war. Furthermore, even before the decade ended it was becoming evident that Canada's ability to produce such goods as newsprint, cars and wheat exceeded the capacity of home and foreign markets to buy them.

One early sign of trouble was that the 1928 Canadian bumper wheat crop had not been fully sold when the 1929 crop was ripening in the fields. Another was the softness of newsprint prices: too many mills had been built and were producing too much paper. A third was a growing number of unsold houses, a sign that those Canadians who wanted and could afford houses already had them. Wild speculation in North American stock markets in the late 1920s was a further indication that it was time for an economic correction. That correction began in the late summer and unforgettable autumn of 1929.

REVIEW AND DISCUSSION

Key People and Ideas
Explain the importance of each of the following as they are discussed in the chapter.

R.B. Bennett   Relief Camp Workers' Union
Arthur "Slim" Evans   "On-to-Ottawa Trek"
Babe Ruth   "The dirty thirties"
Al Capone   "The roaring twenties"
     Dominion Relief Camps

Analysing the Issues
Answer each of the following questions, which deal with important issues raised in the chapter.

1. What two important themes of the Depression years in Canada were demonstrated by the riots in Regina on Dominion Day, 1935?
2. What factors suggest that the "roaring twenties" were not as prosperous as Canadians tend to believe?

Questions for Discussion
Think carefully about the following question and discuss the issues it raises.

1. Who was to blame for the riots in Regina on Dominion Day, 1935? Justify your answer, using evidence from this chapter.

2

THE GREAT CRASH
AND THE DEPRESSION

$100 WILL
BUY THIS CAR
MUST HAVE CASH
LOST ALL ON THE
STOCK MARKET

Black Tuesday, October 29, 1929, was the day that sheer panic took over. Wild confusion reigned on stock exchanges all over North America. The volume of shares traded far exceeded what stock brokers and exchange clerks were used to. Right from the opening bell in the New York Stock Exchange (NYSE) the ticker tapes that recorded sales fell behind. Not knowing exactly what was happening, but fearing the worst from the sharp drops in stock prices recorded early in the day, frightened speculators added to the panic. Hoping to get out of the market before they lost too much money, they offered their shares for whatever price they could get.

When the NYSE ticker tape finally wished its readers good night, it had recorded the sale of 16 410 030 shares. This was a record that stood for many years. In Montreal the volume of 500 000 shares was five times larger than usual. On the staid Toronto Stock Exchange, ten times as many shares changed hands as on a normal day. The turnover on Toronto's Standard Stock and Mining Exchange, preferred by speculators, was more than 1.7 million shares, a record volume.

Observers hardly knew whether to marvel more at the huge numbers of shares sold or the large declines in stock prices. Norranda Mines, for instance, opened at $40 per share and closed at $26.75. It had lost a third of its value in a single day! There were other losses just as big.

Background of the Crash

More than any other day, Black Tuesday came to symbolize the stock market crash of 1929, an event that continues to rank among the most important of this century. Part of its significance lies in its demonstration (not the first or the last) that greed breeds folly. "Anyone not only can be rich, but ought to be rich," a vice-president of General Motors said in the late 1920s. Unwarranted optimism of this kind underlay the frantic speculation of the period. Work was too slow and tedious a path to riches. During the great "bull market" that began in 1924 there seemed to be a faster way. Eventually hundreds of thousands of Americans and Canadians borrowed money in order to back their bet that stock prices would keep on rising. Stock exchanges became little more than legalized gambling dens. The 1929 crash showed that what went up could also go down. This often forgotten fact of stock market life cost a lot of people a lot of money.

After the crash, with the 20:20 vision of hindsight, people found it easy to identify the signposts along the road to collapse. The stock markets had been jittery for several weeks. Price levels reached their peaks on September 3, 1929. A major sell-off took place on September 5, and thereafter the markets drifted gradually down. Optimism remained high, but some experts began to warn against "staying in the market" too long.

Share
A share represents ownership of part of the capital stock of a company, the capital stock being the money invested in the enterprise. A large company might have issued ten million or more shares to the public at one or more times for specified amounts of money.

Opposite page:
One of many who found that the fortune they had on paper had suddenly vanished.

The optimism cracked in mid-October. Why is unclear. There were a few signs of an economic slow-down, however, and that may have made some speculators nervous. Whatever the reasons, fear replaced greed as the dominant emotion among stock market traders. Avalanches always begin slowly; when they pick up speed they become irresistible.

During the rising market speculators had happily borrowed in order to increase their share holdings. When their shares gained in value, they had often used the increased value as collateral for additional loans. This allowed them to buy even more shares. However, there was a catch. The loan agreement was that the current market value of the shares should always be at least double the amount of the loan. That was no problem so long as prices rose. When they began to fall it was another story.

On October 18 and 19, North American stock markets, led by the NYSE, showed growing weakness. Over the weekend stock brokers asked some of their clients who had bought "on margin" for additional collateral on the loans they had made from the brokers. Speculators could either deposit additional securities with their brokers, or use cash to repay part of their loans. If they were unable to do either, they had to sell some of their shares. Indeed, a broker was entitled to sell stock belonging to a client if this was necessary to protect the broker's interests.

In October 1929, thousands of speculators found that the leverage that was supposed to help them get rich could also work the other way. Stock prices could go down as well as up, but loans were fixed in amount. As shares went down rapidly in value, many people who had thought they were rich found that much of their wealth had vanished when they tried to repay their debts. Those who sold early generally made money, though probably not as much as they had thought they would. Those who did not sell early, and many speculators did not, lost heavily.

The avalanche of selling speeded up during the week of October 21. On Thursday, October 24, there were several hours of panic that began on the NYSE and spread to all other markets in North America. Among them were the Grain Exchanges in Chicago and Winnipeg, where prices dropped steeply during the morning's trading. "In ten minutes of ill-treatment, the battered market grovelled before the lash of the seller," a Toronto *Globe* correspondent reported. The prose was purple by today's standards of financial reporting. The reality was shocking enough, however. Many small speculators were ruined by a drop in price of 10 cents per bushel on a contract of 5000 bushels.

The markets rallied towards the end of the day. In New York the "organized support" for the market that speculators had been hoping for appeared at last. Representatives of the largest banks bought stock openly. This reassured many people: prices recov-

Bull Market
*A bull market is one in which the dominant mood is optimism and share prices are rising. Its opposite is a **Bear Market**, in which prices are falling.*

Margin
Margin is the proportion of the price of shares paid by investors and speculators who are buying on credit. The unpaid portion is a loan from the stock brokerage firm.

ered somewhat and held strongly through Saturday morning, October 26. The real disaster began two days later. On Monday there was no more support. The bankers met and announced that they hoped the market would be orderly, but that they would not try to support any particular level of share prices, or protect anyone's position. The avalanche, which had apparently come to a halt, rolled on once again, crushing many in its path.

After the climax of selling on the twenty-ninth, Black Tuesday, stock markets recovered briefly. John D. Rockefeller, the wealthiest man in North America, had told the press: "Believing that the fundamental conditions of the country are sound, . . . my son and I have for some days been purchasing sound common stocks." There was encouraging news about corporate profits. Noting that many stocks were trading at or near their lows for 1929, bargain hunters moved in. Prices went up briskly on October 30 and 31.

The recovery did not last long. In the first two weeks of November there were renewed and sickening declines. By the middle of the month, when prices levelled off once more, stocks on the NYSE had lost, on average, 30 percent of their value in three weeks. This represented a loss, on paper, of $26 billion dollars. Losses in Montreal and Toronto were much smaller in amount but very similar in proportion. Many people had lost a lot of money. Some, who had pledged their homes or other property in doomed attempts to meet margin calls from their brokers and hold on to their shares, had lost everything they owned.

Leverage
Leverage is the advantage gained from using borrowed money to buy shares when prices are increasing. Shares valued at $2000 bought on a margin of 50 percent require the investor to put up $1000 while he borrows the remainder. Should the share value go up by half, to $3000, the investor will have doubled his own investment (minus the loan interest and brokerage fees), provided he sells at this point. The negative aspect of leverage is that if the share value goes down by half, to $1000, the investor will have lost his original investment.

Myths and Facts About the Crash

One myth about the crash that survives even today is that "everyone played the market." That is simply not true. American statistics reveal that no more than 5 in 100 adult Americans had accounts with stock brokers in 1929. Of the 5, moreover, not all would have been speculating or buying on margin. It is unlikely that the situation was very different in Canada. Most Canadians lacked either the money or the inclination to speculate. Playing the market was very largely limited to well-to-do men, and a few women, who were willing to take risks.

A good example was a man who later became prime minister of Canada. Louis St. Laurent, a Quebec City lawyer, had a large portfolio of speculative common shares, bought on margin, at the time of the crash. According to his biographer, St. Laurent's assets "were transformed into almost useless pieces of paper, and his potential wealth into obligations. The fruits of years of hard labour were wiped out; he had to begin again." It took him years merely to repay the debts he had incurred during the speculative boom.

Another myth must also be laid to rest. It is widely believed

Form 6102, replacing Form 2A-T.W.

CANADIAN NATIONAL
TELEGRAPHS

HEAD OFFICE, TORONTO. ONT,   W. G. BARBER, GENERAL MANAGER

Exclusive Connection
with
WESTERN UNION
TELEGRAPH CO.

Cable Service
to all the World

Money Transferred
by Telegraph

SERVICE DESIRED

Day Message
Day Letter
Night Message
Night Letter

Patrons should mark an X opposite the class of service desired; OTHERWISE THE MESSAGE WILL BE TRANSMITTED AS A FULL-RATE TELEGRAM

RECEIVER'S NO. | TIME FILLED | CHECK

Send the following message, subject to the terms on back hereof, which are hereby agreed to

Montreal, Oct. 29, 1929

N.L.T.

Clark Martin & Co.
    232 Portage Avenue
        Winnipeg, Man.

AT CLOSE TONIGHT YOUR ACCOUNT REQUIRES FURTHER THIRTY THOUSAND DOLLARS

OPINION IS THAT WORST IS OVER BUT SOME LIQUIDATION OF WEAK ACCOUNTS MAY

CONTINUE FOR FEW DAYS LONGER STOP TENDENCY IS FOR BANKS TO EASE ON MARGIN

REQUIREMENTS IN ORDER TO HELP SITUATION PLEASE WIRE IN MORNING WHAT YOU WANT

US TO DO.

MATHEWSON MC LENNAN & MOLSON

Charge M.M. & M.

Telegraph operators across the country worked overtime sending and receiving thousands of telegrams like this one from a Montreal brokerage firm to its Winnipeg client.

that the crash was accompanied by an unusual rash of suicides. The notion persists that large numbers of people, presumably ruined speculators, jumped from windows in New York and elsewhere. The myth lacks all foundation. The evidence indicates that the rate of suicide in October and November of 1929 was *lower* than average in the United States. Eventually, in the early 1930s, the rate of suicide did rise. The Depression had a far more devastating effect on a far greater number of people than the stock market crash did.

The Effects of the Crash

By itself, the crash did not cause the Depression of the 1930s, but it did have a lot to do with the poor performance of the North American economy during the Depression years. The people who lost money in 1929 may have been a minority, but they were an influential one. When this previously well-to-do group, among them many lawyers, doctors and businessmen, took losses, they almost immediately cut down on their own and their families' consumption. Sales of luxury goods of every description declined.

More important was the effect that the crash had even on those who had not lost any money. The stock market had become an important cultural symbol for middle-class Americans and Canadians. If it was going down, many people argued, was this not a sure sign that hard times were coming? And in that case, was it not prudent to save rather than spend, to postpone purchases that could be postponed? Rather than buy a new car or refrigerator, make do with the old one—or even do without. Retailers soon felt the pinch of falling sales.

More important yet is what the crash did to business confidence. Business activity depends on the expectation that the goods and services that companies offer for sale will in fact find buyers. The crash undermined that expectation. Not only was the falling stock market a negative signal in itself, it also alerted businessmen to other negative signals in the economy and predisposed them to cut down on production. This led to increased unemployment, which in turn further weakened sales. The optimism of the late 1920s turned to pessimism. Falling business confidence bred prophecies of decline that to a large extent fulfilled themselves.

The Depression and Its Causes

The key economic factor of the Depression was deflation, a major decline in prices for a whole range of goods. This was the result of world-wide overproduction and falling demand. Raw materials and semi-processed goods were particularly hard hit. The prices of manufactured goods did not drop as steeply, but demand for them also fell as the world-wide slump deepened.

Export Prices
In 1933 average prices for Canadian exports were only 62.6 percent of what they had been in 1929.

None of this was new. Excess production had periodically led to falling prices, which in turn led to other problems. Banks tightened credit, that is, they lent out less money, resulting in some businesses going bankrupt and others cutting back on production. All this threw people out of work and tended to depress the wages of those who kept their jobs. In theory at least, such a downturn was cyclical: in due time, once wages had dropped sufficiently and inventories had been reduced, production would begin again and recovery would take place.

In fact, economic slumps had proved increasingly devastating in the nineteenth century, particularly to the urban working classes, and after 1870 they had not been allowed simply to run their course. Great Britain, the strongest economic and financial power, had assumed a responsibility for stabilizing the world economy and following policies that tended to counteract economic downturns. After the 1914–18 war, however, Britain no longer had the strength to stabilize the world economy. The country that had the strength, the United States, did not wish to accept the responsibility. Indeed, as the slump of the 1930s deepened, American policies further destabilized the international economy, making the Depression worse than it would have been otherwise.

The United States reduced imports after 1930, and also reduced investment abroad and at home. This tended to reduce economic activity everywhere. Many Americans thought their Congress and their banks were acting in their country's best interests. They were mistaken. Of all the western countries, only the United States suffered a greater economic decline than Canada.

International Economic Warfare

Some of the reasons for the devastating declines in Canadian production and income were external. Canadian prosperity depended heavily on trade, especially with the United States. International trade declined steadily from 1929 to 1933. Falling industrial activity was partly responsible. Also influential, however, were the barriers that many countries raised against imports, hoping to help their own producers. Policies intended to promote exports were also commonplace. Some of the weapons in the international economic warfare of the 1930s were high tariffs, export subsidies and currency devaluation. Pressured by powerful interest groups and harried by high unemployment, every country tried to improve its own position at the expense of everybody else. This was a struggle that no one could really win, even though some countries scored temporary victories. In the words of one American economic historian: "When every country turned to protect its private national interest, the world economic interest went down the drain, and with it the private interests of all."

An early and heavy blow to Canada was the American Smoot-Hawley tariff of 1930. Its sharply increased duties on farm products hurt ranchers in Alberta and dairy farmers in central Canada, who depended on access to the American market. Increases in American duties on lumber and metals in the early 1930s damaged Canadian forest and mining companies, notably in northern Ontario and northern Quebec as well as New Brunswick and British Columbia.

Canada quickly joined the parade of countries that raised customs tariffs. As a result, some jobs in the manufacturing industries were saved that otherwise might have been lost. However, higher tariffs did nothing for the export industries, such as forest products, mining, fishing and agriculture.

Among the export industries none suffered more than wheat farming. World prices for wheat were very low throughout the 1930s. Argentina, Australia, the United States and the Soviet Union competed with Canada in trying to market their crops. At the same time a number of European countries raised their tariffs in order to protect their own farmers. To make matters worse, there was a drought in southern Saskatchewan that lasted for ten years and annual plagues of grasshoppers. As a result of all these adversities the net money income from farming on the prairies fell disastrously. In Saskatchewan, hardest hit by the combination of natural and man-made calamities, net money income from farming in 1932–33 was only 1.5 percent of what it had been in 1928–29! Total income in the province was little more than a quarter in 1933 of what it had been five years earlier.

Banks
The American banking system, fractured into many small units, was weak throughout the 1920s. The inability of many banks to satisfy depositors who panicked and wanted to withdraw their money led to a severe crisis in late 1932 and early 1933. No Canadian bank failed in the 1930s.

The effects spread far beyond the borders of Saskatchewan. When the movement of wheat to Europe slowed, the railways earned less. They responded by cutting jobs and reducing their purchases of such goods as rails and boxcars. This caused distress and unemployment in the railway car and steel industries, chiefly in Ontario and Cape Breton. The lower volume of freight threw longshoremen out of work in Vancouver, the Lakehead and Montreal. Corporate profits dropped, and companies reduced or eliminated dividend payments to their shareholders. Some companies went into bankruptcy.

Wheat was not alone in having to cope with difficult world markets. In addition to higher tariffs on forest products, the collapse of the construction industry in the United States greatly harmed the lumbermen of British Columbia and New Brunswick. A world-wide glut of pulp and paper had harsh consequences for Canadian paper mills and those employed in them, chiefly in Quebec, Ontario and British Columbia. Low prices for base metals and coal, also in oversupply, caused mines all over the country to reduce their output or close down altogether. Low prices for fish, and restrictions on imports of Canadian fish in several countries, hurt the economies of the Atlantic provinces and the west coast. Wherever profits fell and unemployment rose, even those who continued working felt the pinch. Retailers, tradesmen, professionals, civil servants: all saw their incomes fall.

In the first quarter of 1933, industrial activity in Canada was only 57 percent of the 1925–29 average. The volume of exports in 1933 was 64 percent of what it had been in 1928, up to that time the peak export year. The volume of imports in 1933 was a mere 43 percent of the volume in 1929.

Domestic Causes of the Depression

The Depression was not simply imported from abroad. Some of the causes of the economic distress of the 1930s were home-grown. These included pre-Depression patterns of investment, the heavy burden of debt carried by both the private and the public sectors, and government policies that were too often inappropriate and ineffectual.

There were major surges in domestic investment before the 1914–18 war and in the 1920s. In several industries, among them pulp and paper, railways, automobiles and construction, there was by 1930 significant over-investment and excess capacity. Further opportunities for profitable investment were few. Even after recovery in the mid-1930s was underway, the existing plant and equipment in many industries were enough to satisfy the demand for goods. As a result, unemployment stayed at a high level in the construction and capital goods industries.

One legacy of the earlier investment booms was heavy debt. In order to increase productivity, farmers and business corporations had borrowed large amounts, expecting that future growth would make repayment relatively easy. When growth turned into decline, however, the debts grew ever more heavy. They imposed rigid costs: interest had to be paid annually or semi-annually and

Mackenzie King had been prime minister through most of the twenties. The day after the stock market crash, he confidently claimed that "business was never better, nor faith in Canada's future more justified." Six months later he was still insisting that there was really no need to worry about unemployent. Canadians worried anyway—and stunned King by giving his Conservative opponents a majority in the 1930 election.

there were commitments for repayment of the principal. The amounts of payment were fixed. Prices and incomes fell, but the debt charges stayed the same. Small wonder that Canadians began to complain about the crushing burden of debt.

More than four-fifths of the money that farmers and corporations had borrowed had come from abroad. Much of it was ultimately payable in New York, in American currency. This feature caused financial leaders and politicians to avoid policies that might weaken the Canadian dollar, such as a lowering of interest rates. These remained high in the early 1930s.

Canadians got a taste of currency devaluation in 1931 when Britain went off the gold standard. In the aftermath the Canadian dollar increased in value against the pound sterling, but dropped about 20 percent against the American dollar. The former made Canadian goods more expensive in Britain and associated markets, such as the Commonwealth and Scandinavia. The latter made them more competitive in the United States, although tariffs offset much of this advantage. What the Canadian financial community and governments noticed most, however, were the additional costs of servicing their debts in American currency. For every dollar of interest that was due, most Canadian corporate borrowers now had to come up with as much as $1.25. The additional cost seemed to outweigh the advantages that devaluation brought to companies exporting to the United States.

The commitment to maintain, as far as possible, the value of the Canadian dollar in relation to the American dollar was probably a mistake. It resulted in the loss of markets, particularly for farm and forest products, to competitors such as Australia, New Zealand, Norway and Sweden which devalued their currencies in a determined effort to maintain exports.

Also questionable, though understandable, were the desperate efforts by governments to balance their budgets. The belief in the virtue of a balance between current income and current expenditure was a matter of largely unexamined faith. It was based on a false analogy between a family budget and public accounts. In both cases, many people thought, it was proper to borrow only to acquire capital goods. That might be a house or refrigerator in a family's case, or a canal or bridge in the government's—things from which a long-term benefit might be expected. To go into debt for current expenses was held to be a bad thing.

When income from taxes began to fall after 1929, governments saw only two possible courses of action. They could raise taxes, or they could cut expenses. They tried to do both. From 1926 through 1930, total taxes levied by all governments averaged between 16 and 17 percent of national income. By 1933 they were 26.5 percent! Although governments took a larger share of the national income, they did not have more money to spend. With national income down by almost half from 1929 to 1933, the dollar income of governments was also down. They responded with policies of severe restraint. Education, highways, the armed forces—these and almost all the other functions of government felt the axe of the budget cutters.

Many of the cost-cutting efforts of government, like many of the tax increases, made the Depression worse. They often threw people out of work and cut incomes. This reinforced what was happening in the private sector. And in spite of the cuts, budgets did not come into balance. Governments at all levels found that certain expenses continued to increase, above all the cost of unemployment relief, but also interest on government debts.

The Burden of Public Debt

During the 1920s, provincial and municipal governments had gone into debt for things like roads, bridges, sewer systems, public buildings and schools. The federal government had borrowed heavily to help finance the war effort. In the aftermath of the war, it had supervised the formation of the Canadian National Railways system, and guaranteed the large debts inherited from the pre-existing railway lines.

Having to pay interest on the CNR's debts whenever the rail-

Taxes
All kinds of taxes rose, on income, expenditure and real estate. User fees and licenses also went up. All but the first of these tax burdens tended to weigh more heavily on the poor, who usually spent all they earned.

way's operating income was not enough proved to be Ottawa's most costly responsibility. As the CNR's income fell, the government's expenses rose. The railway's annual operating deficit for the years 1931–33 was $111.4 million. At the time, this was a huge sum of money, being more than a third of Ottawa's current income from taxation. As well, the interest on its own debts took more than a quarter of Ottawa's current income. In the fiscal year 1933–34, all interest charges, for its own debts and those of the CNR, were 61.6 percent of the federal government's total revenue. Small wonder that Ottawa was quite unable to balance its budgets during most of the 1930s! Fortunately it maintained its high credit rating in world money markets and had no trouble borrowing to cover the deficits.

	Total Revenue	Total Interest Charges	Interest Charges as Percentage of Total Revenue
	($ millions)		
Ottawa, fiscal 1933-34	323	199.7*	61.6
Provinces, fiscal year ending in 1933	160.7	55.6	34.6
Municipalities, 1932	373.8	76.7	20.5

* Including CNR deficit of $59 million, calendar year 1933.

Interest charges loomed less large at the provincial and municipal levels, though they were still burdensome. For these governments, however, it was the cost of unemployment relief that made budget-balancing impossible after 1930. A minor item in the public accounts in 1929, relief expenditures rose steeply thereafter. Plagued by difficulties in collecting property taxes, many municipal governments had to turn to provincial governments for the money to make relief payments to unemployed people. In turn, several of the provinces had to borrow money from Ottawa. Having exhausted their own credit, they had to rely on a government whose credit was still good.

In 1930 the total debt of all three levels of government in Canada was $6.2 billion. Although many people already felt this to be heavy, governments were forced to add another $1.7 billion in debt from 1930 to 1937. Little if any of this represented an investment in bold or innovative projects. By far the largest part of it resulted from unavoidable expenses that outstripped income. The deficits were in part the cost of keeping unemployed workers

Relief expenditures by municipal and provincial governments combined totalled $97 million in 1934; the federal government spent a further $60 million.

and drought-stricken farmers alive. To only a very limited extent were they intended, or used, to create jobs.

The deficits were also in part the cost of servicing debts incurred earlier. In this aspect they intensified the Depression. Many of those who received the interest from government and CNR securities lived outside the country. If they lived in Canada, they tended to save rather than reinvest the money. As more than one economist noted, the Depression was so deep and lasted so long partly because of over-saving. As for the Canadian government, it showed no inclination to tax away these savings in order to finance public works projects that would have created jobs.

They might need relief in order to survive, but what the vast majority of unemployed Canadians really wanted was jobs.

The Recovery After 1933 and the Downturn of 1937

Stock markets recovered after hitting bottom in 1932, and the economy began to improve after 1933. The reasons for the recovery were essentially international. In 1932, some assistance to Canadian export industries came from the Empire Trade Agreements, which encouraged trade within the Empire by means of lower tariffs. More important, however, was a change in administrations in the United States in 1933.

The new president, Franklin Delano Roosevelt, had promised to balance the budget, but once in office he did something much more helpful. The "New Deal" programme he unveiled contained many ideas for economic recovery. Among them were schemes for raising the prices of farm products and for public works programmes that would put people back to work. These schemes were not always consistent with each other, but they were all aimed at stimulating the economy. They gave the impression that exciting things were going to happen. Americans began to regain confidence. The recovery in the United States might have come in any case, but its timing was too closely associated with Roosevelt's coming into office to be entirely coincidental.

Recovery in the United States helped to bring recovery to Canada. Prairie farmers shared but little in it, however. Drought, grasshoppers and low crop yields continued to plague them even when prices began slowly to move up. And as long as wheat farming remained weak, so did related sectors of the economy.

At the same time, other international developments brought unprecedented prosperity to some areas. Rearmament began in several countries, most notably Germany after Adolf Hitler came to power in 1933. Rearmament did wonders for nickel mining and so for Sudbury, Ontario. Nickel was essential for armour-plating, and Sudbury was the source of most of the world's nickel at that time. Other metal mining also began to revive, and gold mining boomed after the American government almost doubled the price of gold in 1934, to $35 per ounce. The gold mining towns of northern Ontario and Quèbec flourished. Exploration in the Northwest Territories led to new gold strikes, and to the founding of Yellowknife in 1934.

By 1937 levels of production and corporate profits had regained their 1929 levels in many industries. Prairie agriculture lagged, however. Prices were still well below those of the later 1920s, and unfavourable weather brought the worst wheat crop failure yet. Many workers also failed to share in the recovery. Ten percent of the Canadian workforce was still unemployed, and wage rates had not recovered to their pre-Depression levels.

The recovery was thus far from complete when a new downturn began in 1937. The main reason seems to have been a reduction in public works spending in the United States, and an ill-ad-

One ounce is 28.349 grams.

vised attempt by that country to balance its budget at last. Stock markets fell, business activity declined once more and unemployment rose, in the United States and in Canada. For the next few years Canada's economy was in the doldrums again. Full recovery did not come until well after the outbreak of the Second World War. Tragic as that conflict was, it nevertheless came as a relief to many Canadians after the miseries of the Depression years.

REVIEW AND DISCUSSION

Key People and Ideas
Explain the importance of each of the following as they are discussed in the chapter.

John D. Rockefeller

Franklin Delano Roosevelt

Black Tuesday

New York Stock Exchange

Toronto Stock Exchange

"Bull market"

Deflation

Public Debt

The "New Deal"

Analysing the Issues
Answer each of the following questions, which deal with important issues raised in the chapter.

1. How did "buying on margin" lead many people to lose great amounts of money on the stock market in October 1929?
2. How did the stock market crash contribute to the poor performance of the North American economy during the 1930s?
3. How did international economic warfare contribute to the Depression in Canada during the 1930s?
4. What factors caused Saskatchewan to be particularly hard hit by the Depression?

Questions for Discussion
Think carefully about the following question and discuss the issues it raises.

1. Which causes of the Depression in Canada do you think were the most significant? Why? Develop your own statement of the economic causes of the Depression of the 1930s in Canada.

3

UNEMPLOYMENT AND RELIEF

In 1933 a young man from Saint John, New Brunswick, wrote a letter to the prime minister.

> I am a married man age 26 with one child and have been working for the last three months for little more than my board and have had to break my home up . . . . I am willing to do any kind of work and any length of time. I sincerely hope that you might have some kind of job that you could offer me so that I may get back with my wife and child.
>
> I am sleeping and eating just wherever I can and I have nearly frozen in this last week looking for a job with the few clothes I have. I have no underwear and I don't care to ask for relief as I think something might turn up and there is poorer people than I who need it . . . .

It was only one of many letters of this kind that Richard Bedford Bennett received. Better than most, however, it expressed the concerns of unemployed Canadians. They did not want to apply for unemployment relief; they wanted jobs. But even badly paying jobs were in short supply. As a result hundreds of thousands of wage earners were forced to ask for relief, to go "on the pogey."

Dealing With Unemployment

Canada was ill-prepared to cope with mass unemployment and its effects. When the Depression began there was no unemployment insurance. Workers were expected to save while they worked in order to tide themselves and their families over periods of unemployment. In the seasonal industries, mostly those that were halted by winter, periodic layoff was a certainty. Extreme poverty often resulted.

Public poor relief varied from province to province. In Quebec it was still handled by church-related agencies. The Atlantic provinces offered relief to the destitute out of taxes paid by local property owners for that purpose. In Ontario and the four western provinces, there was no coherent system for dealing with paupers, people so poor they simply could not look after themselves. Traditionally, however, municipal governments were in charge of poor relief, with the provincial governments acting as a sort of backstop. Local practices varied, but everywhere public poor relief was deliberately ungenerous, providing less income than the wages of the worst-paid jobs. Thus, it was thought, the able-bodied would not seek it so long as any work was available at all. Public relief, then, was a last resort, available only to those who had exhausted all other possibilities and who, through illness, disability or plain bad luck, could not survive without it.

A common view of unemployment into the twentieth century was that some of it was unavoidable and in a way even desirable: unavoidable because a lot of work in Canada was seasonal, and desirable because it helped keep wage rates down. Employers and

Opposite page:
The Single Men's Association parades to a Toronto church service.

most politicians saw the latter as a good thing. It was difficult, under the circumstances, to blame people for being unemployed, though unthinking people blamed them anyway. The failure to provide for oneself and one's family was widely taken to be a sign of inadequacy and moral weakness. The trouble with this attitude was that unskilled and semi-skilled workers seldom earned enough to be able to save against that rainy day they knew would come.

From the late nineteenth century on, a small but growing number of observers argued that badly paid people could not be expected to save, and that unemployment, along with illness, old age, disability and family breakup, had become a major cause of destitution. The Liberal Party platform in the federal election of 1921 contained a resolution calling for "an adequate system of insurance against unemployment, sickness, dependence in old age, and other disability, which would include old age pensions, widows' pensions, and maternity benefits." The Liberals won the election and stayed in office for most of the 1920s, but only with respect to old age pensions was anything accomplished. The provinces were primarily responsible for social welfare services, and during the twenties they were much more interested in economic development than in insuring people against the effects of illness, disability or unemployment.

During the economic boom of the later 1920s few Canadians worried much about the economic decline that was bound to follow. The harsh lessons of previous periods of depression and high unemployment were forgotten or ignored. When in the winter of 1929–30 layoffs began to increase beyond the normal, Canada and Canadians were quite unready.

Growth of Unemployment

Average annual unemployment in 1929 was 4.2 percent. It rose to 12.9 percent in 1930 and reached a staggering 26.6 percent in 1933. In the late winter of that year, traditionally the time of greatest job loss, an estimated 32 percent of Canadian wage earners were out of work.

Different regions, industries and classes of workers had very different experiences with unemployment. Export-oriented areas and companies fared worst. Industries that supplied the export sector with equipment and services also did badly. Mine and mill towns from coast to coast had high rates of job loss. Those who worked on the docks and in construction had always suffered from seasonal unemployment; for many of them the off season now stretched the full twelve months.

Unemployment in manufacturing was higher than in the wholesale and retail trades. The financial and service industries, where women were concentrated, had lower rates of unemployment. This explains why in the workforce as a whole a smaller

proportion of women than men lost their jobs. But within these industries, women were more likely to be laid off than men. Workers in the public sector—civil servants, teachers, policemen, firemen, military personnel—suffered little from unemployment. Almost all, however, saw their salaries cut and cut again.

White-collar workers fared better than blue-collar workers, the skilled better than the unskilled. The young had a particularly difficult time. It was very hard to find any kind of job after leaving school or university. According to a study in 1936, when the recovery was well underway, "almost 20 percent of the boys and more than 30 percent of the girls who left Toronto schools in search of a job were definitely registered as unemployed." It was feared that the real proportion was considerably higher, for it was not known where many of the school leavers were. As for young architects, engineers, doctors, dentists and lawyers, they graduated into a world in which those who could afford to pay for their services had their pick of experienced practitioners. Most young professionals simply could not get started, while a good many older ones found it hard to earn any money from their work.

By the late winter of 1933, hundreds of thousands of Canadians were out of work. On April 1, more than 1 400 000 urban Canadians, wage earners and their families, were receiving direct

The practice of hitching rides in and on freightcars was illegal, and railway policemen were supposed to stop it. Sometimes they made the effort to do so, but there were simply too many hoboes and not enough policemen. Hundreds of thousands of transients travelled throughout North America in this uncomfortable but cheap fashion.

relief: food, fuel, shelter and clothing. This meant that approximately one in every four men, women and children living in incorporated cities, towns and villages depended on public relief to keep from starving or freezing to death. In many places, among them Montreal, Que., East Windsor, Ont., Swift Current, Sask., and Port Alberni, B.C., more than one in three were on relief.

Although the economy gradually recovered after the spring of 1933, many Canadians continued to depend on relief, particularly during the winter. A first bout of unemployment usually exhausted whatever savings a family might have. A renewed layoff then forced them to apply for relief almost right away. The average rate of unemployment in 1936 was 16.7 percent; in March of that year no fewer than 1 250 000 urban Canadians were on direct relief. In March of 1939 there were still 700 000 urban Canadians, or about one in eight, receiving direct relief. The numbers describe an appalling disaster: the pauperization of a large part of the Canadian working class.

Being on Relief

People feared and hated relief. To accept it was an admission of failure and defeat. Working-class people might have no alternative; middle-class people who lost their jobs tried to avoid it, or did not even think they ought to apply. A letter to the prime minister from the wife of a civil engineer is illuminating.

> We have two small boys . . . ; have had to give up our home, sell our furniture, and come to live with my parents, two old people who have barely enough for themselves. We have lived, this past winter, on less than seventy-five cents a day for the four of us, and that given to us by my husband's mother . . . . There is town relief, of course, but we're professional people, we're outside the pale as regards town relief.

Staying with parents or with grownup children, or with other relatives, was the most common way of avoiding having to apply for relief. This way was closed to most working-class people, however. Their relations were generally too poor, and lived in dwellings already overcrowded. People spent whatever savings they might have, pawned as many of their belongings as they could spare and get some money for, borrowed where they could, and tested the limits of their credit with shopkeepers and landlords. Often they got some help in the form of food or hand-me-down clothing from churches or charitable agencies. Beyond that lay the humiliation of applying for relief. This meant proving that you were destitute, and generally brought with it a minute examination of your private affairs. If you still had a liquor permit, for example—something you needed in those days in order to buy alcoholic beverages—you had to surrender it, and probably got a lecture on the irresponsibility of drinking in the bargain.

Once admitted to the relief rolls, families could expect a steady though miserably low income. In 1936 the maximum monthly relief allowance for a family of five averaged $39 in the 45 largest Canadian cities. This amount normally covered food, fuel and shelter, as well as clothing and medical care where it was available. The amounts paid ranged from a low of $18.86 a month in Halifax, which did not pay rent, to a high of $60.60 in Calgary. Even Calgary's relatively generous allowance left a family of five in abject poverty.

In the early stages of the Depression, relief was usually indirect. Adult males were put to work on relief projects, such as road work, ditch digging or clearing snow. This soon proved too expensive, and direct relief became the rule. The notion that people ought to work in order to get relief was not totally abandoned, however. Periodically men had to turn up to perform some menial and generally pointless work, such as digging dandelions out of boulevards. This was called "boondoggling." Those who had to do it hated it, while property tax payers complained about having to pay for it. On the whole, people hated direct relief even more than indirect relief, particularly if it was paid in vouchers for goods rather than in cash. Having to present the vouchers in stores was deeply resented by people who knew it stamped them as reliefers, miserable failures.

In various communities some reliefers organized themselves into Unemployed Workers' Associations and agitated, usually without much success, for more generous relief allowances or for jobs. The authorities did not welcome their efforts. Many people simply sank into apathy, despair or a sullen resentment against "the system." Protest movements and new political parties did spring up, but they never enjoyed the support of more than a relatively small minority of reliefers.

The Menace of Homeless Single Men

In order to limit costs, many communities made it difficult for single young people to get relief in their own right. If they were already living by themselves when they became unemployed, they might be able to qualify, although the municipal authorities preferred them, especially young women, to "go back home." Those who wanted to leave home and applied for relief were turned down. Yet they were often unwilling to remain dependent on their parents. Moreover, conflict often arose out of the presence of young adults with nothing to do. Bored and perhaps believing that the grass was bound to be greener on the other side, many young men, and a handful of young women, took to the roads and rails in search of work and of adventure.

They became part of a growing army of transients, "hoboes" as they were called. They hitched rides from motorists or, much

An RCMP officer in Edmonton said disapprovingly in 1932: "I have seen men come into the office with tears in their eyes suffering humiliation at being forced to apply for assistance, and today the very same men are demanding increases in relief and adopting the attitude that it is their inalienable right to receive relief."

more commonly, travelled in or on railway freightcars. They took casual jobs, begged and, it was feared, sometimes stole in order to survive. "Hobo jungles" sprang up in or near most towns, generally near railway freightyards. On vacant pieces of land the hoboes erected rough shelters, cooked and ate, argued and swapped bits of news and gossip, and slept. There was little point in arresting them for vagrancy: jails were comfortable compared to what they were used to.

In 1931 the federal Minister of Labour drew Prime Minister Bennett's attention to the growing "transient menace." A year later Charlotte Whitton, a social worker who was inquiring into relief administration in the West, advised Bennett that there were more than 100 000 transients in the four western provinces alone. Ineligible for any but the most makeshift kind of relief because they were not resident anywhere, they were beginning to organize and demand services. "They are generally becoming a menace to law, order, property and security," Whitton warned.

Charlotte Whitton
Charlotte Whitton later became the first woman mayor of a Canadian city, in Ottawa in 1951.

Ontario and British Columbia had already established work camps for transients. Whitton urged Bennett to open federal camps as well. Somewhat similar advice reached the government from General A.G.L. McNaughton, Chief of the General Staff of the Canadian Army. He worried that Communist organizers were finding fertile ground among the hoboes, and feared that this might lead to violence. He suggested that the army might be able to play a role in preventing disorder.

Late in 1932 Ottawa established its own camps, and placed them under the penny-pinching administration of the Department of National Defence. In 1934 McNaughton boasted that the total cost per man-day of relief in the camps had been only $1.17 in the period from November 1, 1933 to March 31, 1934. This included every conceivable expense.

The federal relief camps expanded rapidly. Entrance into them was voluntary, but local governments did their best to encourage men into them by cutting off relief to single men or by ending all assistance to transients. Once in the camps, men were not treated badly. The accommodations were spartan but usually clean. The meals were unimaginative but ample. Clothing was sturdy, and of better quality than most of the men had seen for months or even years. Discipline, though strict, was far from brutal. Yet the camps were unpopular.

One big problem was that none of the planners seemed to have given any thought to recreation and culture in the camps. Eventually some church groups interested themselves in the matter, and sent books and magazines as well as board and card games. Frontier College sent volunteers to offer some opportunities for education. But much of the time the inmates were bored.

Another problem was that the daily allowance of 20 cents

Opposite page:
After signing into a federal relief camp, a man could count on not going hungry and on having a roof over his head. There would be little in the way of comforts or entertainment, however, and still less to give him any hope of a more meaningful and better future.

was regarded as insultingly small. Most important, however, was that the camps were obviously holding places for young men for whom the economy and the country had no use. An editorial in the Vancouver *Province* commented:

> The mistake the government is making is in treating these young men, just on the threshold of life, as though they were old men . . . . In an old people's home, good shelter, good food, good clothing and a little pocket money are boons . . . . But to build young men's lives on the model of old men's homes and to suppose that young men will be satisfied with the things that delight the old is to betray a woeful misconception of the psychology of youth. The young man has ambitions, and urges. He wants to be out and doing.

He wanted to start a family, to have a home of his own. The camps offered no prospect of anything better, however. They led nowhere. This contributed to feelings of hopelessness and despair. Among some, it led to demands for change, for "work with wages." This was the background to the relief camp strikes and the On-to-Ottawa trek.

Another dramatic confrontation between unemployed men and the authorities took place in Vancouver in 1938. Cutbacks in provincial relief funding led to the virtual elimination of assistance to transients. In protest, hundreds of men occupied the Art Gallery and the Central Post Office and staged what was then called a sit-down strike (a sit-in, it would be called now). After some days they left the gallery quietly, but continued to occupy the post office until police used clubs and tear gas to drive them out. After this bloody encounter, the transients staged an On-to-Victoria trek. The municipal government put them up in vacant warehouses while negotiations took place. Eventually the trekkers scored a modest success: the federal government undertook to pay the cost of relief for non-resident transients in British Columbia.

Governments and Relief Costs

Low as relief payments were, they soon strained the budgets of many municipalities. Like private charitable organizations, local governments found that they could not cope with the increased demands for assistance. They turned to provincial governments for help, and by 1931, the provinces were looking to Ottawa.

The federal government grudgingly provided grants and loans to many municipalities and provinces, while also spending money in its own right. In a special session of Parliament in 1930, the newly victorious Conservatives passed a $20 million relief works act. A year later they followed this with the Unemployment and Farm Relief Act, which authorized Ottawa to spend additional sums of money in fighting the Depression.

Although Ottawa ended up providing much of the money

Hear the Reply of the authorities to Strikers' Delegation requesting immediate Relief and opening of negotiations on counter-proposals to Bennett Government's offer of Concentration Camps

MASS MEETING TONIGHT
Market Square 8 p.m.
(If wet will be held in Stadium)

Several Speakers representing local organizations will address the crowd

Winnipeg Strike Camp situation will be outlined. Latest developments will be given

Strikers' Funds are Completely Depleted

Support the Strikers and Force the authorities to grant immediate Relief

Poster announcing the July 1, 1935 strikers' meeting in Regina.

Police armed with clubs and tear gas evict strikers from Vancouver's Central Post Office.

that provincial and municipal governments spent on relief, the federal government refused to take any responsibility for administering it. That seemed likely to be both expensive and politically unrewarding. In fact, no one wanted the responsibility, so it stayed with the municipalities. They cried for "relief from relief," but they were stuck with it.

The costs of relief increased steadily even as income from property taxes fell. Many people were simply unable to pay these taxes. Local governments made agonizing efforts to cut expenses: they cut the salaries and number of their employees, stopped the construction of buildings and roads, and postponed routine maintenance and repairs. Such policies of extreme restraint threw even more people out of work, while cities and towns began to take on an ever shabbier appearance. In spite of heroic attempts to adjust to declining tax revenue, however, scores of municipal governments were unable to pay the interest on their debts.

This fate also threatened several provincial governments, and in 1936 the province of Alberta actually went into default by failing to make a payment of interest on its debt. The other western

Newfoundland entered Canada as the tenth province in 1949.

provinces were bailed out by the federal government. Newfoundland—still a self-governing Dominion at that time—was less fortunate. It saw tax revenues plummet even as growing numbers of Newfoundlanders were forced to apply for relief. Heavily in debt as a result of borrowing for railway construction, the government of Newfoundland found in 1932 that its credit was exhausted and that it could not pay the interest on its debt. A commission of inquiry, on which Britain and Canada as well as Newfoundland had representation, recommended that the Dominion abandon self-government and allow itself to be governed by a British-appointed Commission, one of whose objectives would be to re-establish Newfoundland's credit. The Legislature accepted this recommendation, and Newfoundland lost self-government.

Problems for the Future

Policies of restraint added to the problems of the present by adding to unemployment. They also stored up difficulties for the future. Postponing necessary maintenance was bound to lead to increased expense a few years down the road. But politicians defended themselves against criticism by pointing out that they simply did not have the money to do what needed to be done. It was for this reason, too, that few people in government discussed the possibility of unemployment insurance during the early Depression years. The provinces did not have the money, and it was widely believed, at least before 1935, that Ottawa could not act alone. Belt-tightening did not manage to balance budgets, but both municipal and provincial governments felt strongly obliged to try to tighten their belts.

If some Canadians worried about the long-range consequences of restraint in public spending, others worried about the effects of long-term unemployment, particularly on young people. How were youngsters to learn steady habits of work if they could not find their first jobs?

Also worrying was the trend to long-term dependence on relief. Charlotte Whitton, in particular, felt troubled by a growing tendency "to seek relief and to stay on it." In January, 1939, with the unemployment rate over 15 percent, she suggested that the greatest threat to Canadian well-being "now lies . . . in the letdown of spirit and morale in the country." Unfortunately, the general public, the taxpayer, and the recipient of aid alike seem to be settling down to an attitude that relief is here to stay."

Whitton overstated the case. The great majority of unemployed Canadians wanted to work. It was not their fault that there were not enough jobs. It may well be true, however, that to some of the unemployed, life on the pogey, however miserable, was no worse and possibly better than the menial, fitful and badly paid work they had once had.

In the late 1930s Leonard Marsh, an economist at McGill University in Montreal, also warned of dangers ahead. A tenth of Canadians were drifting into chronic dependence, he wrote. Unemployment was the chief cause, and working-class people were its main victims. "Unemployment drags men down;" it led to loss of skills, and a lack of skills "increased the risk of inferior employment and frequent layoff."

The Second World War masked what was happening for a while. But after the war Marsh's fears turned out to have been well-founded. A "welfare trap" was taking shape. A study of welfare recipients in 1971 found that more than a quarter of them were the second generation in their families to be dependent. They were one of the tragic legacies of the Depression.

REVIEW AND DISCUSSION

Key People and Ideas
Explain the importance of each of the following as they are discussed in the chapter.

Charlotte Whitton

General A.G.L. McNaughton

Leonard Marsh

"On the pogey"

Public poor relief

"Boondoggling"

Unemployed Workers' Associations

Hoboes

"Transient menace"

Relief Works Act

Unemployment and Farm Relief Act

Analysing the Issues
Answer each of the following questions, which deal with important issues raised in the chapter.

1. What was the common attitude of Canadians during the 1920s towards unemployment and the unemployed?
2. What groups of Canadians were the hardest hit by unemployment during the 1930s?
3. What factors made "going on relief" so humiliating?

Questions for Discussion
Think carefully about the following question and discuss the issues it raises.

1. Should the Bennett government have done more for the unemployed during the Depression or would this simply have increased the "welfare trap"? What about today? Do you think governments in Canada do too much for the unemployed or should they do even more? Explain your answer.

4

AGRICULTURE AND
THE CRISIS OF "KING WHEAT"

The land was as lifeless as ashes, and for miles there was scarcely a growing thing to be seen. Where a scanty herbage had struggled up through the dust, flights of grasshoppers had apparently completed the destruction and then, despairing of other sustenance, had flown off to other fields . . . .

Gaunt cattle and horses, with little save their skins to cover their bones, stalked about the denuded acres . . . . The few people in evidence in the little towns seemed haggard and hopeless. For fully 50 miles of the region traversed by the highway which bears the ill-omened number of "13," there did not appear to be one single field that will produce a bushel of grain or a load of fodder.

The reporter for the *Regina Leader-Post* who wrote this account of southeastern Saskatchewan in July 1934, added that the livestock would have to be moved or feed would have to be shipped in. "And as for the people themselves, God only knows what their extremity must be . . . . The land upon which they have depended for sustenance has utterly failed them."

Few images of the Depression in Canada are more powerful than the duststorms of drought-stricken Saskatchewan. Certainly the addition of drought to other problems hit Saskatchewan farmers particularly hard, but farmers everywhere in Canada suffered from low prices and the shrinking of foreign markets.

Farmers and Fishermen

For farmers and fishermen, as for other producers of primary goods, the deflation of the early 1930s was a disaster. Between 1929 and 1933 average prices for farm products dropped by almost half. During the same period the average price of the goods and services used by farmers fell by only a quarter. As a group, therefore, Canadian farmers saw their standard of living go down by 25 percent in four years.

Of course the growing poverty of farmers did not affect them and their families alone. As they stopped buying things they could no longer afford, many other Canadians—from shopkeepers in small prairie towns to factory workers in central Canada—felt the consequences. Approximately three in ten Canadians still made their living from agriculture, and they constituted an important part of the Canadian market. Whether the things made or offered for sale were farm tractors, automobiles, appliances, ready-made clothing, books or life insurance policies, if farmers bought less of them, others could not help but suffer as a result.

As a group, only the fishermen of the Atlantic provinces had as bad a time of it as farmers. At the depth of the Depression in 1933, average export prices of Canadian fish were half of what they had been four years earlier. The price of dried cod, a key product of the Atlantic fisheries, was at one point down by almost

Opposite page: Thousands of farm families left the drought-stricken southern prairie and trekked north to start life over on primitive farms in the park belt.

Canadian farmers were hit
hard by the American
Smoot–Hawley tariff of
1930:

**Value of Exports
to the United States
($ millions)**

	1929	1933
Cattle	13.8	.4
Potatoes	3.8	.7
Milk and cream	5.7	.04

*From Renfrew, Ontario,
another farmer wrote: "I
am greatly in need of help.
I have 9 of a family. We
are living on a farm, but
haven't made enough to
even pay our back taxes.
The children have over two
miles to walk to school,
they haven't the clothing
to go now that the cold
weather is setting in . . . .
I haver never applied to
anyone for anything
before, but we surely need
it now."*

70 percent. At the same time other countries imposed new tariff barriers that made it harder to market Canadian fish.

The Atlantic fishing industry had been in bad shape even before the Depression began. The catch was usually ample, but incomes were not. Fishermen had to deal with a small number of companies that bought and distributed fish. They had little bargaining power, for there was heavy competition among them and little real competition among the buyers. During the 1930s even the fish distributing companies (and, in British Columbia, the salmon canneries) suffered serious financial losses as markets shrank, but ultimately, it was the fishermen who suffered most. The total annual marketed value of all fish landed in Nova Scotia, New Brunswick, Prince Edward Island and the Magdalen Islands of Quebec was $19.3 million in 1929. In 1933 it was down to $10.3 million. In the fishing villages poverty had always been commonplace. During the early 1930s it became extreme.

Farm poverty also increased in the Atlantic provinces. The cash income of farmers there had never been high; by 1933 it had all but vanished. On the other hand, many farm families were able to supply themselves with food to eat and firewood to burn. So long as they were not in debt, farmers in central Canada, British Columbia and the Maritimes were generally able to get by. Indeed, in these areas the rural population actually grew during the 1930s. Drought and low wheat prices forced thousands of farmers off the land in the prairie provinces, but elsewhere the drift into towns and cities came to a temporary halt. Rural poverty was miserable, but it was usually easier to bear than destitution in the towns and the demeaning experience of applying for relief.

Debt, however, was a burden that crushed or came close to crushing many farmers in all parts of the country. Among the thousands who wrote Prime Minister R.B. Bennett were many poor farmers. A letter from a Quebec farmer was in many ways representative: "I am writing to see if you could tell me any way I could get some help or if there is any loans I could get as I have a mortgage and am in bad need of some help as I have a family of 8 children all small and I am going to lose my place."

The Dethronement of "King Wheat"

Rural distress was greatest on the prairies, and it was greatest of all in Saskatchewan, beset by years of low prices as well as significant declines in yields and production. Low prices were an international phenomenon over which neither the farmers nor the Canadian government had any control. The declines in yield and production were the result of insect pests, plant disease and bad weather—above all drought.

Drought affected many parts of the prairies during the 1930s, but it had its most devastating impact on southwestern and south-central Saskatchewan, the area known as Palliser's Triangle. This semi-arid region had been opened to the plow after 1907, at a time when rainfall was higher than usual. Unfortunately rainfall from 1929 through 1937 was low, and the land dried out. High winds then blew away the topsoil. Farming techniques that might have limited the damage were not yet in widespread use, and many careful, competent farmers were quite unable to fend off the combined effects of drought and wind. Dust storms and soil drifts became common features of rural life.

The year 1928 was the last good one that many prairie farmers had for more than a decade. Prices were not particularly high, nor were the grades of wheat, but crops were huge. Saskatchewan farmers alone harvested a record 321 million bushels.

The crop in 1929 was little over half the size of 1928's, and, what was worse, the price dropped steeply in the autumn and continued to fall. Surpluses exported from Australia, Argentina, the United States and the Soviet Union, added to the Canadian exports, all helped to depress world prices of wheat. The average price per bushel had been over one dollar as late as the summer of 1929; it was a dismal 35 cents in 1932. Similar declines in price hit everything else the western farmer produced: oats, barley, rye and flax. The ranchers of Alberta, who had seen cattle prices average $42 a head in the late twenties, had to accept an average of $24.83 a head during the first half of the 1930s. Prices for sheep, hogs, butter and eggs dropped from 40 to 60 percent and more.

In spite of these low prices, animal products became more important in the prairie economy. This was partly because the low prices for oats and barley encouraged many farmers to raise more livestock, and partly because wheat was a disappointing crop throughout the 1930s. In Saskatchewan, the most important wheat province, yields from 1929 through 1938 were persistently below average. In Alberta and Manitoba the results were only slightly better. Saskatchewan produced a mere 37 million bushels in 1937, and all three provinces only 159 million bushels.

Gross farm incomes dropped steeply. Farm expenses fell far less. As a result, the net income of prairie farmers by 1933 was only 8 percent of what it had been in 1928. Saskatchewan farmers fared worst of all. Before the Depression they had, as a group, been the most prosperous of Canadian farmers. In the 1930s they became the poorest.

The average Saskatchewan farmer in 1928 enjoyed a net cash income of $1614. This allowed him to pay family living expenses such as clothing, fruit and vegetables, tea, coffee and cocoa, sugar and salt, life insurance premiums, doctor's bills, school books, magazine subscriptions, telephone bills, gasoline for the family car and so on, as well as holidays, and perhaps to put aside some savings. That same average farmer had net cash income of

Net income from agriculture in Saskatchewan was $228.4 million in 1928, but only $3.5 million in 1933. Some of this was the result of the drought in southern Saskatchewan, but the very low prices for farm products made it very difficult even for farmers with good crops to make a profit.

only $66 in 1933. This meant abject poverty. Some sample prices from the mid-thirties drive this point home. A dozen oranges were 33 cents; a pound (454 g) of sugar was 5 cents, a pound of coffee 39 cents, a pound of tea 66 cents. Women's shoes cost from $4 to $15 a pair, men's shirts started at $2, a pair of children's over-shoes was 65 cents. Soap was 5 cents a bar, toothpaste 25 cents a tube. A book cost from $1.50 to $5, an inexpensive radio $30. A refrigerator was $100 to $200, a new Ford coupe $645.

Farm families cut down drastically on all cash purchases. New clothing became an unattainable luxury. Houses fell into dis-repair; furniture and kitchen utensils were not replaced when they broke. Automobile registrations fell by approximately one half, as did telephone subscriptions.

Rural isolation increased dramatically as a result. "Consider a farmer's financial straits when for $10.50 a year he will do without a telephone," an observer wrote in 1931. "Perhaps he is 10 or 15 miles from town, perhaps a mile from his nearest neigh-bour, yet for the sake of that paltry sum, he will face the hazards, the isolation, the social inconvenience of doing without his tele-phone. I think this more than anything else shows our western financial position." Of course, $10.50 was far from a "paltry sum" to someone whose annual cash income was less than $100.

Going into the thirties, almost half of prairie farmers had cars, but now there was often no money for gas and oil, to say nothing of repairs or replacement. And so the "Bennett buggy" appeared: an automobile body, stripped of its engine and drawn by a horse. It was a telling symbol of impoverishment in an area that had prospered not long before.

Also telling were the letters that reached Prime Minister Ben-nett from prairie farmers or, more commonly, their wives. Many

A Bennett buggy, ox-cart style. More commonly horses pulled the non-functioning automobile.

of these dealt with clothing. A farm woman west of Saskatoon wrote in 1933:

> Please send for the underwear in the Eaton order (made and enclosed in this letter). My husband will be 64 in December . . . . I have patched and darned his old underwear for the last two years; but they are completely done . . . . We have never asked for anything of anybody before, we seem to be shut out from the world altogether—we have no telephone, radio or newspaper . . . . If I can only get this underwear for my husband I can manage for myself in some way. He has to be out in the cold, where I can stay in the house.

From Cando, farther north in Saskatchewan, a farm woman with three children explained in 1935 that her husband had lost his farm in the south when a mortgage company had foreclosed.

> We are now on a quarter [section] of brush land. We are living in a 1 ply, 1 room shack. There is no roof except tar paper, and every time it rains our bedding is soaked . . . . Every cow we owned died last winter, also my chickens. My children are barefooted, as well as myself. The shack we live in is so cold already, I pile all the rags I can find on the beds and yet we freeze. What will it be like when winter really comes?

Food was the most basic issue. Before the Depression the typical farm household on the prairies supplied itself with 40 to 50 percent of its food needs. Leafy vegetables and fruit were in short supply, and ready cash had to be used to buy them. When the 1930s came even farm families outside the drought area generally had to make do with no more than those vegetables that they could grow in whatever gardens they had. In the drought area any contribution that a family could make to feeding itself soon dwindled or even vanished.

The Saskatchewan Relief Commission
Very soon after 1929 rural municipalities in much of southern Saskatchewan found themselves unable to cope with relief funding. Income from property taxes dwindled while the number of destitute farm families grew. No longer able to borrow, the municipalities turned to the provincial government for help.

In 1931 the widespread failure of the wheat crop put the funding of relief beyond Saskatchewan's financial resources. Like municipal revenues, provincial revenues were falling. Income from tax sources such as gasoline and liquor decreased as people cut back on non-essential spending. At the same time relief expenditures continued to grow, and even ruthless cuts in other government programmes did not suffice to keep the budget in balance. The province's bankers were unwilling to provide loans that the province might not be able to repay. What was to be done?

The province looked to Ottawa for help and got a sympathetic hearing. The federal government knew that a catastrophe was taking shape and agreed to subsidize provincial relief of rural destitution. In August 1931, the provincial government appointed a special agency, the Saskatchewan Relief Commission, to administer the emergency aid to farmers. For the next three years it did a ruthlessly efficient job. By 1933 it was responsible for 200 000 human beings.

Before being admitted to relief, a farmer had to complete an application designed to determine precisely how great his need was. The application passed through local relief officers and district relief committees to the Commission in Regina. On the single criterion of need, the applicant would receive any combination of food, clothing, fuel, fodder and seed. In every case the applicant had to undertake to repay the relief when able to do so. The Commission hoped in this way to remove the stigma of charity from the relief it supplied. Little was ever repaid.

Maximum economy was a prime goal of relief administration. Any hint that a farmer might be getting more than he really needed was enough to prompt an investigation. If a farmer still drove a car, the Commission withheld relief until convinced that the car was essential. The purchase of any alcoholic beverage was enough to get one removed from the relief rolls. Small wonder that many relief recipients saw the administration as intrusive and humiliating.

Another Commission goal was to disturb the normal features of rural life as little as possible. Goods were generally supplied through local shopkeepers, thus enabling many of them to stay in business where otherwise they would have failed. The government subsidized physicians and dentists, so that they could cover necessary expenses and enjoy some minimal income. The Commission supplied fuel to many schools and paid direct relief to teachers when school boards could not afford their salaries. The teachers were supposed to repay this relief once the school boards paid their back salaries. (A lot was never paid.) Had the Commission not acted, doctors and dentists would have been forced to leave for want of patients who could afford to pay them, and many school districts would have been without teachers altogether.

Almost two-thirds of the $35 million that the Commission spent in its three years of life went to maintain farming operations. Thus it supplied feed, fodder and seed grain, and made loans for harvester repairs, binder twine, barbed wire and so on. In these various ways the Commission helped to keep people in southern Saskatchewan who otherwise would have had to leave.

Some special problems also became the responsibility of the Commission. Hundreds of families from the drought-stricken south and others seeking an alternative to being on relief in one of

the cities received support to resettle in the wooded area of northern Saskatchewan. Life there was primitive and those who went
were usually dirt-poor. The Commission had to provide food,
tools and seed as well as clothing and building materials.

In late 1932 the Commission assumed the administration of
relief for transient single men. Many were put to work on farms,
with the farmer providing room and board and the Commission,
using federal government funds, paying the worker $5 a month.
Single women were put to work as domestic servants on the same
terms. Men for whom no farm work was available were encouraged to enter federal relief camps. On the whole, men seem to
have preferred farm work, even though it paid slightly less than
work in the relief camps. Farm work at least had some evident
purpose and value, and it was not supervised by the Department
of National Defence.

The Commission came to an end in 1934, regretted by few
who had been subject to its supervision. A provincial election
brought a Liberal victory and a new government, headed by J.G.
Gardiner. It transferred responsibility for rural relief to various

No one who
experienced the
duststorms of the
thirties ever quite forgot
them. Decades later,
one prairie resident
recalled:

"[The land] just picked
up and blew across the
countryside. You look
out and see this great
cloud of dust coming
and then you're in it and
you can hardly see . . . .
The grit gets into your
nose and mouth and
into the houses, drifting
in under the doors."

As a group, only the fishermen of Atlantic Canada suffered as greatly as prairie farmers. Their incomes did not fall as dramatically, but they had been barely adequate before.

government departments, with some minor savings as a result. This regime pinched pennies as its predecessor had but seemed to relent a bit. The Commission, for instance, had permitted no purchases of fruit at all, or of vegetables other than potatoes and dried beans. The Bureau of Public Welfare, which succeeded the Commission in administering direct relief, allowed such purchases while warning that the total food allowance must not be exceeded.

Under neither regime was the food allowance generous. The Relief Commission in 1933–34 allowed $10 plus one 98-pound (44-kg) bag of flour every month for a family of five. The Bureau of Public Welfare allowed $13.15 per month in 1935, $16.50 in 1936, and $20.20 in 1937. However, these amounts had to cover flour as well as other food purchases. Moreover, the Bureau made deductions of up to 25 percent where families had private supplies of meat, dairy products or potatoes.

In southern Saskatchewan malnutrition became commonplace, particularly among children. In 1937 doctors reported cases of scurvy, caused by a lack of fresh fruit and vegetables. Startled by this, the federal government distributed 782 boxcars of fruit, vegetables, cheese, fish and beans in the drought areas. This was the official counterpart to what had been happening privately for years, as church groups, welfare agencies and generous individuals sent help. The two railway companies contributed by waiving freight charges on donations. Charity of this kind relieved the misery only temporarily, but it was nonetheless most welcome.

Debt and Its Adjustment

Debt was a serious problem for private companies as well as governments. It was even more serious for farmers. In 1933 the House of Commons Select Standing Committee on Banking and Commerce reported that "out of a total of 654 297 owned and partly owned farms, 244 201 were mortgaged to the extent of $677 564 100." The Committee did not state how many farmers owed how much for crop loans and chattel mortgages on farm machinery. Reasonable estimates place total farm indebtedness at between $750 million and a billion or more.

Farmers might have borrowed to buy their land, to expand their farms, to buy equipment or farm animals, or to put in a crop. Whatever the reason, those who had borrowed now found that interest costs swallowed an ever larger portion of the income from the sale of their products. They could seldom make up for the declines in price by producing more, so their incomes dropped while their interest costs were fixed. Eventually many farmers were unable to pay the interest on their debts and their creditors foreclosed, either selling the farm in order to recover the money owing to them, or taking it over. As a result thousands of farmers became tenants on land that they had previously owned. In Saskatchewan almost 10 percent of those who had owned their farms in 1931 had lost them by 1936.

Some of the farmers who got into debt trouble in the 1930s had recklessly overextended themselves in the preceding decade. Most were in no way to blame for their difficulties, however, and as the number of foreclosures increased farmers began to pressure governments to help them. In the early 1930s seven of the nine provinces passed debt adjustment legislation. (The exceptions were New Brunswick and Prince Edward Island.) This legislation typically dealt with the debts of selected individuals, notably farmers, by establishing a moratorium, a temporary halt, on payments of principal and interest. The idea was that the debtors would resume paying as soon as they were able to, and in the meantime could not be forced off their land.

Even in the prairie provinces the legislation did not provide for a compulsory reduction of debts or interest charges. Moreover, provincial measures did not prevent a piling up of unpaid interest and thus of new debt. Not surprisingly many farmers demanded laws that would force a reduction of debts and interest rates. If a decline in prices reduced farm income and made farmland less valuable, the farmers argued, why should the price of money, in the form of interest rates, not be cut and debts reduced in size? Prairie legislators sympathized with the argument and the demand, but most of them believed (and they were probably right) that a forced reduction of debts was beyond their power under the British North America Act.

Interest Rates
Interest rates for farm mortgages stayed at 6 to 7 percent into the middle 1930s. In view of the reality of falling prices, these rates were ruinously high.

They had other misgivings as well. They respected private property and the sanctity of contracts. To scale down debts without the agreement of the creditors seemed like theft. How willing would lending institutions in the future be to lend money in a province that had unilaterally reduced the size of debts or interest rates?

It was common to paint the lending institutions, banks, trust, mortgage and life insurance companies, as soulless machines, or as vampires that sucked the farmers' lifeblood. Mostly with head offices in central Canada, they were particularly unpopular in the West. Their managers, farmers charged, refused to recognize the changed economic circumstances of the Depression.

Such criticism was understandable but misplaced. The managers had legal obligations to the shareholders of their companies and to their own lenders. Trust and mortgage companies had borrowed heavily abroad in the 1920s in order to satisfy the demand for credit in Canada. They owed money for long terms and at fixed rates of interest. They could scarcely agree to major reductions in the money owing to them without getting similar concessions from their own creditors. Such concessions were not forthcoming. In their absence, reductions of debt and interest rates within Canada would have undermined the soundness of Canadian financial companies.

Farmers did not care about the details of international and domestic borrowing or high finance. Faced with a mounting debt load and afraid that they would never get out from under it, they saw mortgage company officers and bankers as well-dressed, well-fed menaces. They felt helpless and exposed, and they wanted relief from their debts.

Ottawa finally helped indebted farmers in 1934. By this time Prime Minister Bennett had come to the conclusion that the federal government's power over bankruptcy and insolvency gave it the right to force an adjustment of debts. The result was the Farmers' Creditors Arrangements Act, which provided for the compulsory cutting of "both interest and principal down to the productive level of the farm." Financial institutions challenged the act's constitutionality in the courts. In 1937, the highest court in the British Commonwealth, the Judicial Committee of the Privy Council, found it to be *intra vires,* that is, within the legislative competence of the Dominion government.

Farmers commonly complained that the process of debt adjustment under the Farmers' Creditors Arrangement Act took too much time. Nevertheless, in its first four years of operation the act was used to deal with 26 000 cases, covering farm debts totalling $158 million. The resulting reduction in debt was $50 million, almost a third, and the cut in interest payments was some $4.2 million. Some farmers had reason to applaud the act.

Ottawa and the Farmers

The Farmers' Creditors Arrangement Act was only one of several federal government initiatives on behalf of farmers. The government of R.B. Bennett passed other acts, at least two of them of lasting significance. The most sweeping piece of legislation was the Natural Products Marketing Act of 1934. Farmers generally welcomed this act, which established a Dominion Marketing Board with powers to regulate the movement and direct the sale of a long list of products, including meat, wool, wheat and timber. Large sectors of the Canadian economy would thus have come under federal supervision and direction, but the Judicial Committee of the Privy Council judged it in 1937 to be *ultra vires,* or beyond the government's power.

More specifically directed to the grain trade was the Canadian Wheat Board Act of 1935. At the outset of the Depression the wheat trade was in private hands. Wheat growers' co-operatives, the Pools, marketed more than half of the wheat grown in 1928–29; privately owned elevator companies marketed the rest. The Pools took responsibility for selling their members' wheat in an orderly fashion, with a view to obtaining the best price possible. They paid their members an advance, with a further payout once the crop had been sold.

The initial payment for the 1929 crop year was $1 a bushel, which seemed reasonable—even low—when it was announced. With the collapse of the international price of wheat in the fall of 1929, however, the Pools were suddenly in trouble. They had borrowed from the banks in order to make the initial payment to

Across southern Saskatchewan, abandoned farmhouses bore silent testimony to the devastating effects of the combination of man-made and natural disasters that hit the prairies in the thirties.

their members, but now could not realize from sales the money necessary to repay the loans. An attempt in 1930 to raise the price by withholding much of the western crop failed dismally as grain exporters in other parts of the world brought their crops to market. The prairie governments had to step in to guarantee the Pools' bank loans. The Pools withdrew from marketing, henceforth serving as elevator storage companies.

Late in 1930 the Dominion government gave its guarantee of the Pools' loans, the credit of the prairie provinces being by now very much in doubt. At the same time Ottawa took control of the Pools' marketing machinery. From 1931 to 1935 R.B. Bennett and his grain advisor, John I. McFarland, managed the marketing of the western wheat crop without much consultation with anyone else. Bennett intended the establishment of the Canadian Wheat Board in 1935 as a popular political move. A body with the same name had marketed the crop in 1919–20, and many farmers remembered it fondly. For years they had agitated for its return; in 1935 Bennett finally obliged them. But the Wheat Board delivered less than it appeared to promise.

The most important piece of legislation affecting agriculture was the Prairie Farm Rehabilitation Act (PFRA). Passed in 1935, it provided "for the rehabilitation of drought and soil drifting areas in the Provinces of Manitoba, Saskatchewan and Alberta." Journalist James Gray has written that the PFRA was "one of the great Canadian success stories of all time. Yet it is completely unknown to 99 out of 100 Canadians." With the personnel of the five regional Dominion Experimental Farms, the three university Faculties of Agriculture, and the provincial Departments of Agriculture playing key roles, men and women set out to reclaim the near-desert of the southern plains. New farming techniques, such as strip-farming on a two-year rotation of grain and summer fallow, came into use. Scientific soil surveys helped the PFRA decide what land could be reclaimed for growing grain and what should be reserved for grazing. One early result was the establishment of community pastures. Barbed wire fences were built around the first wastelands intended for pasture in 1937. Eventually 80 000 cattle would graze on 800 000 hectares of grassland that had once been wind-blown desert. Irrigation projects soon took shape as well, a few of them large, most of them small. Another important project was tree planting.

Gradually the efforts of many people served to reclaim much of the dry land. Increased rainfall after 1937 also helped: the drought was finally at an end. Without the dedicated work of prairie men and women, however, rain alone could not have restored the arid south. In a decade that was difficult for all farmers and catastrophic for many, the PFRA stands as an inspiring monument to positive achievement.

REVIEW AND DISCUSSION

Key People and Ideas
Explain the importance of each of the following as they are discussed in the chapter.

J.G. Gardiner

John I. McFarland

Palliser's Triangle

The Saskatchewan
   Relief Commission

The Bureau of Public Welfare

Debt adjustment legislation

Farmers' Creditors
   Arrangements Act

Prairie Farm Rehabilitation Act

Analysing the Issues
Answer each of the following questions, which deal with important issues raised in the chapter.

1. What were the factors which led both farmers and fishermen into poverty during the 1930s?
2. What factors made debt such a problem for farmers during the 1930s?
3. What actions were taken by the federal government to assist farmers during the Depression?

Questions for Discussion
Think carefully about the following question and discuss the issues it raises.

1. What were the good and bad sides of the Saskatchewan Relief Commission? Do you think the Commission offered a satisfactory solution to the problem of poverty in Saskatchewan? Use specific evidence from the chapter to support your point of view.

5

GOVERNMENT AND POLITICS

Prime Minister William Lyon Mackenzie King was annoyed. Opposition M.P.'s had suggested he make grants to the provinces to help them to deal with growing unemployment. Why should his government subsidize the provinces? Why should Ottawa raise tax money that the provinces would get to spend? Let them increase their own taxes!

Particularly galling was the thought of giving cash to the five Conservative provincial governments: Nova Scotia, New Brunswick, Ontario, Saskatchewan and British Columbia. "So far as giving money from this federal treasury is concerned," he said, ". . . I might be prepared to go a certain length possibly in meeting one or two of the western provinces that have Progressive premiers at the head of their governments, but I would not give a single cent to any Tory government."

There was a storm of protest from the Opposition benches. "Shame," cried the Conservative leader, R.B. Bennett. "Shame," others echoed. "What is there to be ashamed of?" Mackenzie King asked, and then rubbed it in: "My honourable friend is getting very indignant. Something evidently has got under his skin. May I repeat what I said? With respect to giving moneys out of the federal treasury to any Tory government for these alleged unemployment purposes . . . , I would not give them a five-cent piece."

It was April 3, 1930. That evening King regretted his outburst. He knew that he was right where the Constitution was concerned: Ottawa at that time had no responsibility for unemployment. However, he realized that his remarks could be used to make his government look callous and unconcerned. Then he looked at the bright side. Most people were employed and would not benefit from federal grants to the provinces in any case. His remarks might even "appeal to the people," he wrote in his diary.

He was mistaken.

The Conservatives in Office

A federal election took place on July 28, 1930. King's Liberals ran on their record since 1926. They had lowered taxes; the country had prospered. The budget of 1930 promised improved trade with other British Empire countries. Unfortunately for the Liberals, the prosperity of the late 1920s was fading rapidly. Just as bad, the Liberal party machinery was in disrepair. The party and its leader had given insufficient thought to finances and organization. The Conservatives, on the other hand, were ready for an election. Their party was well financed; thousands of members stood ready to help it take advantage of the Liberals' weakness. They cleverly exploited the deepening economic slump. Farmers were unhappy about declining prices, businessmen about falling profits, workers about growing unemployment. King's "five-cent

The Progressive Movement
The Progressive movement, active in promoting rural interests and values and supported mainly by farmers, became active in politics during and immediately after the First World War. It had considerable success at the provincial and federal levels both in Ontario and on the Prairies. In 1930 Manitoba still had a Progressive government, while Alberta was governed by the United Farmers of Alberta, another wing of the movement.

Opposite page:
Richard Bedford
Bennett, a wealthy
Calgary lawyer who
exuded confidence, led
the federal Conservatives to victory in
1930.

Election of 1930

Party	% Share of Popular Vote
Conservative	48.8
Liberal	45.2
United Farmers and Progressive	2.8
Others (Labour; Independent)	3.2

speech'' came back to haunt him: the Tories would not allow Canadians to forget.

King was nevertheless confident that his party would win. Instead the Conservatives took 137 seats out of 245, a gain of 46 seats, while the Liberals took only 91, a drop of 25. The United Farmers of Alberta elected 9 members, but elsewhere the Progressives all but disappeared. There were also 3 Labour and Socialist members, most notably James Shaver Woodsworth from Winnipeg North Centre.

Had good intentions and energy been enough, the new government might well have pulled Canada out of the Depression. However, the $20 million in relief works voted in a special session of Parliament was little more than a drop of water on a hot stove. As for the higher tariffs that the government introduced, they were of limited value. During the election Bennett had made the questionable promise that higher tariffs would serve to ''blast a way into the markets of the world.'' The rest of the world was not impressed, however, and did not lower their tariffs when Canada raised hers. What the higher tariffs did do was help the manufacturing industries save profits and jobs, mostly in Ontario and Quebec where these industries were concentrated. They also increased American investment in Canada as firms that could no longer export profitably to Canada bought up Canadian factories in order to manufacture inside Canada for the Canadian market.

In addition the tariffs reinforced a situation that existed in any case. The prices of manufactured goods fell considerably less than those of natural resources. The outlying regions, whose economies were dominated by export-oriented resource industries, suffered more from the Depression than did southern Ontario and Quebec. This increased the sense of grievance among farmers and other primary producers. It also added to the tension that existed between Ottawa and some of the provincial governments, particularly those of Alberta and British Columbia.

Federal government policies from 1930 to 1934 were unimaginative. Ottawa launched some relief projects, including the work camps for single men, and made grants and loans to the provinces in aid of unemployment and farm relief. It also tried, with very modest success, to secure markets for Canadian products. Its main concerns, however, were to protect Canada's credit rating by trying—in vain—to balance the budget, and to preserve so far as possible the Canadian dollar's value in relation to the American currency. The second of these concerns in particular reinforced the destructive effects of deflation on the resource industries. It made it harder for them to compete with the products of countries that devalued their currencies in the early 1930s.

Ottawa's policies tended to favour the well-to-do. Those who gained their income from investments rather than from work were, as a group, considerably better off in 1933 than in 1929. They certainly took a larger share of the national income, while the shares taken by farmers and fishermen dropped dramatically.

The Bennett "New Deal"

By 1934 the Conservatives were beginning to change their course. The Natural Products Marketing Act and the Farmers' Creditors Arrangement Act were signs of a new attitude. The Bennett government had become readier to intervene in economic life.

One important reason for this was the falling prestige of businessmen. They had dominated the 1920s but had clearly failed to solve the problems of the Depression. Along with the loss of confidence in businessmen came a rising faith in political leadership.

This new faith found particularly malignant expression in Germany. There, after 1933, Adolf Hitler and his National Socialists sought to impose their twisted vision of the future. In the United States a more benign presence asserted itself. Elected in November 1932, President Franklin Delano Roosevelt took office the following March. He was the first American president to become genuinely popular north of the border, and his "New Deal" soon excited Canadian observers. Here at last was a leader who was willing to experiment with new policies in an attempt to end the Depression.

One convert was R.B. Bennett's brother-in-law, W.D. Herridge. He recognized that the Roosevelt New Deal's underlying purpose was to make the capitalist system function more effectively and humanely. He also saw the New Deal's popularity. From his vantage point as Canadian Minister (the equivalent of today's ambassador) in Washington, he began to urge Bennett to introduce something similar in Canada.

Herridge made his views public in a speech to the Canadian Club in Ottawa on December 15, 1934. "If we made business less our religion and religion more our business," he said, "if we proclaimed by deeds the eternal truths of the Christian faith, we might find that this [capitalist] system did not work so badly after all." He did not want to rely on individual regeneration alone, however. "If in the economic system there are faults inherent in the system or perpetuated by the selfishness of a class; if they are correctible neither automatically nor through the unassisted efforts of the individual, what possible redress remains? The State!" He denied that interference with the profit system led inevitably to a loss of rights: "Reform will do far more to save the system than ever will stubborn protests of its inviolability."

Public reaction to Herridge's speech was generally favourable. From Oxbow, Saskatchewan, one Conservative wrote to Bennett in fervent support of Herridge. The capitalist system badly needed changing: "The process of pumping prosperity in at the top, and expecting it to percolate to the bottom, has failed to work here, as elsewhere . . . . Why not try pumping some prosperity in at the bottom, and see if it won't percolate upwards?''

Bennett made his move in early January. In a series of radio broadcasts he announced a programme of reform. With economic recovery underway, he explained, the time had come to correct the imbalance of power between capital and labour. Workers would get protection previously denied them, including contributory unemployment insurance, a uniform minimum wage, an eight-hour day, a maximum work week, and health insurance. There would be closer regulation of business corporations and higher taxes on investment income.

Bennett's programme was inspired largely by Roosevelt's New Deal, but in defending it, Bennett emphasized British examples and the need to counter the political left. To a company president he wrote: ''Even if we are able to give full effect to all our proposals we will still be a long way behind Great Britain in social reform.'' He told a Conservative M.P.: ''It is clear that we must make a determined thrust forward or our country will fall into the hands of the extreme left.'' Contrary to what some seemed to think he had not become a socialist, he responded to one supporter: ''But I do propose to enact such legislation as will ensure the more successful operation of the capitalist system.''

Bennett, who had himself profited greatly from the capitalist system, had no intention of abolishing or weakening it. Like Herridge, however, he was a staunch member of the United Church of Canada, and he accepted a personal responsibility for the welfare of others. Indeed, while he was prime minister he received thousands of requests for money and answered many of them. How much he gave away is not known, but it must have run into the tens of thousands of dollars. He was, furthermore, deeply loyal to Britain. That the Mother Country had enacted certain social reforms was bound to impress him. At the same time he was a politican who knew that he faced an election in 1935. Years of depression had made his government unpopular. A reform programme seemed one way of restoring its chances of victory.

There were those, mainly businessmen, who thought the programme unconstitutional, unnecessary or even harmful. Others supported it in principle, but argued that it went too far. Bennett answered charges that his New Deal was beyond the legislative power of the federal government by referring to Ottawa's power to make treaties. His proposal was to put into practice a number of conventions of the International Labour Organization, of which Canada was a member. Of more concern to him were complaints that the New Deal went too far, for many of these came from longtime supporters of his party. The legislation actually put forward was less radical than the radio speeches had suggested it would be. All the same, among the New Deal statutes passed were ones providing for unemployment insurance, minimum wages, maximum hours of work, and a weekly day of rest. There were also the Canadian Wheat Board Act and the Prairie Farm Rehabilitation Act. A Conservative government had become the most reformist that Canada had so far seen!

The Election of 1935

Bennett led a disorganized party into the election held on October 14, 1935. Some Conservatives questioned the value of the New Deal. Others doubted the quality of Bennett's leadership. Bennett was able and energetic, but in trying to carry out his ideas and policies he was often autocratic, tending to value his own judgement far more highly than that of others. He ran what usually seemed like a one-man show. Reluctant to delegate authority, he overworked himself and by 1935 was quite exhausted. For some weeks in the late winter he was in the hospital, and in his absence the government drifted.

Winnipeg Free Press cartoonist Arch Dale's version of Bennett's one-man-show style of government.

Continued unemployment and low prices for the products of resource industries undermined Conservative support. Bennett had allowed the party machinery to fall into disrepair. Even worse, some members had left the party and founded their own. The Reconstruction Party was the creation of Harry H. Stevens, Bennett's Minister of Trade and Commerce until late 1934.

In January that year, Stevens had started preaching that some large firms, particularly in retailing and processing, had too much power. He did not oppose large firms if they encouraged efficiency, he told an audience on January 15. "But I do object to such powerful organizations being used for the purpose of crushing or eliminating their individual competitors." Stevens believed small businessmen to be "properly the finest expression of democratic life anywhere," and his sometimes intemperate attacks on large enterprises displeased several of his cabinet colleagues. Furthermore, a personal rivalry developed between him and Bennett. His position in the cabinet having become increasingly difficult, Stevens finally resigned and decided to launch his own political party. Bennett's New Deal, he charged, did not go far enough.

Two other new parties contested seats in the 1935 election. One was the Co-operative Commonwealth Federation (CCF). Founded in 1932, it consisted of groups of radicalized farmers, assorted small labour parties, and middle-class people organized into CCF clubs. Their leader was J.S. Woodsworth, since 1921 a Labour M.P. from Winnipeg. The party's programme, known as the Regina Manifesto because it had been adopted in Regina in 1933, was socialist in tone and content. It called for the nationalization of banks and many other large enterprises. It also looked to an increase in co-operative activity, greatly expanded social ser-

*The Regina Manifesto was
drafted by a few members
of the League for Social
Reconstruction, an
organization of
intellectuals which was
founded in 1932 and which
was a major source of
reformist ideas in the
1930s. Among its leading
members were University
of Toronto historian Frank
Underhill, who did the
first draft of the Regina
Manifesto, and McGill law
professor and poet Frank
Scott.*

Election of 1935

Party	%Share of Popular Vote
Liberal	44.8
Conservative	29.6
Social Credit	4.1
CCF	8.8
Reconstruction	8.7
Independent and United Farmers	3.9

vices, and a wider measure of economic and political equality in Canada. The other new political entity was Social Credit. Most of its support was in Alberta, and there at least it promised to give the major parties a real run for their money in the federal election. A much less important challenge came from the small Communist Party of Canada.

The main threat to the Conservative government was Mackenzie King's Liberal party. Patient and careful, the pudgy King had bided his time. In the years since 1930 he had overseen the improvement of party finances and organization, while resisting demands from some of its members that it become more reform-minded. A sometime social worker and labour relations consultant, King was not averse to reform. However, he distrusted proposals for change that seemed to him to exceed either the electorate's hopes and wishes or the constitutional powers of the Dominion government. He was not as flamboyant as Bennett, and he was certainly less generous, but he had a better sense of what was politically feasible. Convinced that Bennett's victory in 1930 had been a fluke and aware of the grave difficulties that the Depression had created for the governing party, King waited with some confidence for his own return to power. It was "King or Chaos," Liberal campaign posters in 1935 proclaimed.

This time, King's optimism was justified. Not that many more people voted Liberal than in 1930. What happened was that the Conservatives' vote collapsed. They won only 40 seats. The Liberals actually suffered a small decline in their share of the popular vote but nearly doubled their number of seats, to 173.

Smaller parties and independents took more than a quarter of the popular vote. The CCF had contested 118 of the 245 seats and won 7 of them, in Manitoba, Saskatchewan and British Columbia. The Reconstruction Party had entered 174 candidates but only one was elected, Harry Stevens himself. Social Credit showed the advantages of concentrating a party's strength in one region. It limited itself to 45 candidates, mainly on the prairies. Seventeen of them won their seats, 15 in Alberta and 2 in Saskatchewan. Five Independent Liberals, one Independent, and one United Farmers of Ontario–Labour candidate were also successful. The last of these was the redoubtable Agnes Macphail, who had represented Grey–Bruce in Ontario since 1921.

Provincial Politics

At the provincial as at the federal level, the appearance of political change was greater than the reality. Only one provincial administration, that of John Bracken in Manitoba, managed to survive the Depression without defeat.

In the Atlantic provinces, Conservative governments were overwhelmed by a Liberal tide. In Nova Scotia the able and charismatic Angus L. Macdonald led the Liberals to a sweeping victory in 1933. Two years later in New Brunswick the administration of L.P.D. Tilley met crushing defeat at the hands of A.A. Dysart's Liberals. Prince Edward Island voters turned the Liberals out in 1931, but four years later gave them all 30 seats in the provincial Legislature.

In Saskatchewan, J.T.M. Anderson headed a coalition of Conservatives and Progressives that had gained office in 1929, narrowly defeating J.G. Gardiner's Liberal government. After an election five years later the Conservatives, the dominant force in the coalition, were left without a seat. Gardiner's resurgent Liberals took 50 seats, and were opposed only by a small band of 5 members from the Farmer–Labour Party, the Saskatchewan wing of the national CCF.

In Manitoba, John Bracken's Progressives played the coalition game with skill. Bracken's policies were cautious and financially conservative. Except for the costs of unemployment relief, which ballooned in Manitoba as they did everywhere, his government was able to balance the budget. This it accomplished by a combination of high taxes and severe cutbacks in spending. These policies might have led to its defeat, but before the 1932 election the pragmatic premier managed to forge an alliance with the provincial Liberals. This produced a handsome victory. In the 1936 election Bracken's coalition paid a price for its inability to end the

The parliamentary caucus of the CCF and its secretary in the late 1930s. From left to right: T.C. Douglas, Angus MacInnis, A.A. Heaps, J.S. Woodsworth, M.J. Coldwell, Grace MacInnis, Grant McNeil.

Depression: it lost 15 seats and its majority in the Legislature. However, a post-election agreement with the 5 Social Credit members who had been elected kept Bracken in office.

British Columbia

The only province in which the defeat of the Conservatives led to a major shift in policies was British Columbia. Thomas Dufferin Pattullo, an Ontario-born businessman, led the Liberals to victory in 1933. The Tories collapsed completely and the young CCF became the Opposition. "Unemployment is destroying self-reliance and self-respect," Pattullo charged during his campaign. His party promised a programme of "work and wages." Pattullo's "Little New Deal" was quite radical, in fact. He wanted better old age pensions and state health insurance. He also wanted Ottawa to take full responsibility for unemployment or else to vacate the income tax field. This, he argued, would allow a province like British Columbia to fund reform programmes.

Pattullo's relations with Bennett were unhappy, and his relations with King were no better. He opposed the policies of restraint followed by both prime ministers. Unable to borrow in its own right after the early 1930s, however, British Columbia had to depend on Ottawa for money. This weakened the province's bargaining position as well as its freedom of action. Lack of money, as well as the hostility of many physicians, forced Pattullo to abandon a scheme of provincial health insurance, the first in Canadian history, even though a majority of voters had approved it in a plebiscite. The Liberals lost four seats in the provincial election in 1937, and the Conservatives replaced the CCF as Opposition. Pattullo became less inclined to push for social reforms. He did, however, become even more stubborn than before in his defence of provincial rights.

William Aberhart and Social Credit

Another staunch defender of provincial rights was Alberta's William Aberhart. In the provincial election of 1935 his Social Credit movement won a landslide victory, defeating a government tainted by scandal and discredited by its inability to cope with drought, low prices and unemployment. It is safe to say that few of the Albertans who voted Social Credit knew what the movement stood for. A controversial economic doctrine developed by a Scottish engineer, Major C.H. Douglas, Social Credit held that in modern economies the ability to consume always fell short of the capacity to produce. The result, Douglas said, was economic depression. Social Credit would correct this depression by means of a monthly "social dividend," to be paid to all adults. By maintaining consumer purchasing power, this would presumably prevent future depressions.

Agnes Macphail was the first woman elected to the House of Commons. She held her seat from 1921 until 1940 and later became one of the first two women to sit in the Ontario legislature.

Economists and bankers generally dismissed Social Credit as mistaken and unworkable; lawyers and political scientists pointed out that creating money was beyond the legal power of provinces. Nevertheless Aberhart, a respected Calgary high school principal and radio evangelist, gained support. He denounced "poverty in the midst of plenty," attacked the deflationary policies of the federal government and the financial institutions, and promised "just wages," "just prices," and the reduction of farm debts. More important than any of these from the voters' point of view, he held out the promise of the social dividend. As a farmer from central Alberta later said, "You can strip down the appeal of Social Credit to the $25 a month. All of us farmers were in desperate straits. Here was William Aberhart promising $25 a month, and he was a minister of the Gospel."

Aberhart's attempt to put the Social Credit programme into action came in 1937. Several provincial acts sought to regulate banking and other financial institutions. The federal government reacted quickly, challenging some of the acts in the courts and using its constitutional power to disallow others. This power had not been used for 14 years, and Aberhart was incensed. "It was never the intention of those who drew up whatever constitution we may have, that men and women who . . . are potentially the richest people on earth, should live lives of insecurity, privation and hardship year after year," he complained to Mackenzie King. King was unmoved. The BNA Act clearly assigned responsibility for money and banking to the Dominion government. Ottawa could not tolerate Alberta's attempt to invade this field.

It thus became clear that most of Social Credit's financial and economic ideas, whether one believed them beneficial or not, simply could not be put into effect in one province alone. Awareness of this sapped whatever radicalism the movement originally had. Social Credit in Alberta became a rather conservative movement. Its hostility to Ottawa, however, remained strong for years.

William Aberhart led his Social Credit party to victory in Alberta in 1935, promising fair prices, fair wages and a monthly "social dividend" of $25. Few Albertans understood Social Credit, but they trusted Aberhart.

Mitchell Hepburn's Ontario

Another vigorous opponent of Ottawa was Ontario's Liberal premier Mitchell Hepburn. In June 1934 he defeated the competent but dull George Henry. "We are in this thing because of the little fellow," Hepburn told reporters after the election, "the workman who isn't working any more, the farmer who is struggling against unbelievable odds . . . . We're in this thing because of them and for them. There is going to be a new deal in this province."

What this mainly meant in practice was "cheaper government." Soon after the Liberals took office they fired hundreds of civil servants. In August, 8000 taxpayers cheered at Varsity Stadium, Toronto, as the government's 47 limousines were auctioned off. The new government also cancelled contracts to buy hydro-

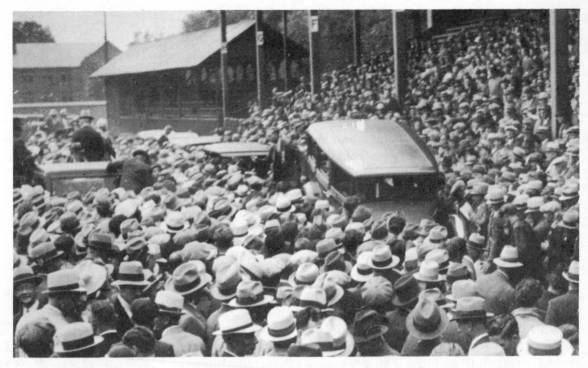

In 1934 at Varsity Stadium in Toronto, Mitchell Hepburn's new Liberal government auctioned off the province's 47 official limousines as an economy measure. They netted $34 000.

electric power from several Quebec companies, power which the province was no longer deemed to need.

Although Hepburn campaigned for the federal Liberals in 1935, improved relations between the province and Ottawa did not follow the Liberal victory. Hepburn and Mackenzie King were both Ontarians and Liberals, but they had little else in common. They did not like each other much. Hepburn was an extrovert who enjoyed partying. Indeed, his growing taste for whisky and women damaged his health and his career. King, in contrast, was a fussy bachelor who rarely took a drink. He did take a dim view of Hepburn's robust tastes. Beyond this, King feared that Hepburn wanted to exercise too much influence within the federal Liberal party. For his part, Hepburn soon became convinced that King was trying to downgrade the status and power of the provinces in general and Ontario in particular.

Accordingly Hepburn was suspicious of the Royal Commission on Dominion-Provincial Relations, formed by the Dominion government in 1937. He suspected that it would recommend transfers of money to the western provinces—money that could only come from Ontario taxpayers, since Ontario was the wealthiest province. "Ontario is going to cast off the role of milch cow for the rest of the Dominion," he warned in 1938. When he appeared before the Commission in May he called for an increase in provincial taxing powers. Later he announced that his government would have nothing more to do with the Commission.

Hepburn's concern for the little man did not translate into

legislation. He was capable of acts of kindness, but he generally opposed the extension of government activity, even on behalf of the poor and down-trodden. He was a rural conservative who thought that social services would hardly be necessary once prosperity returned. His government did pass the Industrial Standards Act of 1935, intended to equalize minimum wages and maximum hours of work throughout the province, but it owed very little to his ideas. His progressive Attorney General, Arthur Roebuck, was responsible for the act, and Hepburn later confessed privately that he himself had never liked it.

Per Capita Income, 1928-29	
Ontario	$549
Canada	471
Quebec	391

Quebec

The Depression increased nationalist feelings in Quebec. These were aimed partly against Ottawa and partly against "foreigners," *les anglais.* Nationalism, the insistence on the special value and mission of French Canada, was nothing new. However, the intense misery of the 1930s gave added strength to that insistence.

In relative terms the Depression hit Quebec no harder than Ontario. In each province the drop in per capita income from 1928–29 to 1933 was 44 percent. But Quebec was poorer to begin with. Even in the comparatively prosperous 1920s about three-quarters of Montreal's working classes lived in poverty. After 1929 things got much worse.

It was easy to blame *les anglais* for the mounting distress. In pursuit of economic growth, Quebec governments had for decades done their best to attract American investment. Regulation and labour legislation were minimal; taxes and wages were low. The attitude of the Liberal government, led since 1920 by L.-A. Taschereau, was that growth would in due time provide prosperity. When that might be no one knew.

Nationalists tended to exalt a rural life and traditional values. They distrusted the cities and sought "a sound balance" between industry and agriculture. Often they were priests; usually their ideals of society and the family were highly conservative. To these men, a woman's place was in the home. Such attitudes were widely shared in Quebec: it was the only province that had not given the vote to women during or soon after World War I.

Foreign investment had always been suspect in the eyes of many nationalists. In the 1930s the leading figure in the nationalist movement was Lionel Groulx, a priest. His organization, *Action nationale,* agitated for French-Canadian ownership of large enterprises and especially of the "electricity trust." The rates charged by Quebec's hydro-electric companies were high; so were their profits. The cost of electrical power became a symbol of all that was said to be wrong with foreign-owned industry.

Business corporations seemed remote, however. Some Quebeckers felt it made more sense to hate *les anglais* who were

Thérèse Casgrain, active in the women's movement in Quebec, played a major part in securing the vote for women in that province. They finally got it in 1940.

closer by. The *Achat chez nous* (buy at our own place) movement saw intellectuals and small businessmen urging French Canadians to buy goods only in French-Canadian shops and to avoid "foreign," particularly Jewish stores.

The Rise of the Union Nationale

As the economy worsened, demands that the provincial government do something about it grew. The government undertook some job-creating public works projects and made grants for unemployment relief, but mainly it looked to the opening up of new agricultural regions to solve the problem of mass unemployment. This "back-to-the-land" or "colonization" movement got the support of the Church as well as of many nationalists. During the 1930s some 45 000 Quebeckers were settled on the farming frontier in the Abitibi, Temiscaming, Lac Saint-Jean, Rimouski and Gaspé regions. Most of the land they occupied was unsuitable for farming, however, and many of them did not stay.

By 1933 a group of young Liberals had become increasingly critical of what they saw as the government's ineffectiveness in the face of the Depression, as well as its friendliness to foreign investors. This group chose the name *Action libérale nationale* (ALN); its leader was Paul Gouin, son of a former Liberal premier of Quebec. Gouin and his associates hoped to "re-liberalize" the Liberal party. The ALN proposed a number of reforms, including the elimination of monopolies such as the "electricity trust," aid to agriculture, a more equal distribution of income and wealth, and an end to corruption in public life.

Taschereau's party showed little willingness to change. In 1935, therefore, the ALN broke with the Liberals and turned itself into a political party. The Conservative leader, Maurice Duplessis, saw his chance. A lawyer from Trois-Rivières and a man of considerable charm, he persuaded Gouin that united their parties might have a hope of defeating the Liberals.

Quebec Election, 1935
Of the UN's 42 seats in 1935, the ALN had 26 and the Conservatives 16.

Just before the provincial election in November 1935, the two men announced "a united front against the common enemy of the people of Quebec, the Taschereau regime." The alliance took the name *Union nationale Duplessis–Gouin* (UN). It scored a near-victory, taking 42 seats to the Liberals' 48. A skilled parliamentarian, Duplessis was soon unearthing scandals and exposing Liberal mismanagement. Taschereau resigned in disgrace in 1936, leaving Adélard Godbout to lead the Liberals into a new election.

Godbout introduced several of the reforms that the ALN had called for, but it was too late. The Liberals were disorganized; the UN ran a strong campaign. Duplessis was by this time its sole leader, Gouin having resigned after charging that his ally was trying to remake the UN into the provincial Conservative party in all but name. Most of the ALN supporters stuck with Duplessis and helped the UN win a smashing victory.

Once in office, Duplessis abandoned most of the UN programme. His government neither tried to regulate private companies nor established a provincially owned hydro-electric system like Ontario's. Government should encourage private enterprise, Duplessis believed, not interfere with it. The UN's promises of social reform went by the board. Only in agriculture did Duplessis fulfill the UN's promises. This was good politics: by 1931 little more than a third of the people of Quebec lived in rural districts, but they elected almost two-thirds of the members of the Legislative Assembly. Budgets for colonization, rural roads, agricultural education and low-interest farm credit all increased. So did projects of rural electrification, though by the end of the 1930s almost nine out of ten Quebec farms still lacked electricity.

The Padlock Act

The best-remembered piece of legislation of the UN's first term in office is the so-called Padlock Act. Officially titled "Act Concerning Communistic Propaganda," it was intended to safeguard the province against an alleged communist threat. The act was one of the most dramatic examples of hostility to the Communist Party of Canada (CPC) during the 1930s. Few Canadians had any use for communists, but before the late 1920s there was little interference with their rights. After the Depression began, however, there was fear in many circles that the CPC would stir up the unemployed. The federal government used the Immigration Act to deport foreign-born communists and other radicals. Several provincial governments used section 98 of the Criminal Code, dealing with unlawful associations and seditious conspiracy, to prosecute communists. In Ontario, in 1931, the secretary of the CPC, Tim Buck, and seven other leading communists were convicted and sent to Kingston Penitentiary.

After returning to office in 1935, Mackenzie King's government repealed section 98. Conservatives generally opposed this, Duplessis among them. One result was Quebec's Padlock Act. It allowed the police to padlock for up to a year any premises they suspected were being used for spreading communistic propaganda. The term "communistic" was nowhere defined, however, and the appeal procedure involved proving one's innocence rather than the police having to prove one's guilt. Beyond this, the Padlock Act interfered blatantly with important civil liberties, freedom of association and freedom of speech. Critics of the act claimed, moreover, that it invaded the field of criminal law, a federal area of responsibility.

Nevertheless the act enjoyed strong support within Quebec. The Roman Catholic Church welcomed it; both English- and French-language newspapers gave it editorial approval. All the members of the Legislature voted for it. Only a handful of people

Defeated in the 1939 provincial election, Maurice Duplessis returned to power in 1944 and remained firmly in control of the province until his death in 1959.

The Padlock Act
The Supreme Court of
Canada finally struck
down the Padlock Act as
unconstitutional in 1957.

joined together in April 1937 to form the Canadian Civil Liberties Union in order to fight the act. In alliance with such groups as the CCF and the League for Social Reconstruction, the Civil Liberties Union urged the federal government to disallow the act or at least refer it to the courts for an opinion on its constitutionality. Unwilling to offend Duplessis, the federal government declined.

There is no doubt that Duplessis would have taken badly to any interference by Ottawa. He very quickly developed into a champion of provincial rights, and in 1937 formed a personal friendship with Ontario's Premier Hepburn. From then on, the two men joined together in opposing Ottawa's initiatives.

The Liberal Way

When Mackenzie King returned to office in 1935, five years in Opposition had not changed his views about the proper relationship between Ottawa and the provinces. He and his Minister of Finance, Charles Dunning, were unhappy about the cost of loans and grants to the provinces for unemployment relief. Neither wanted to spend Ottawa's tax revenues for provincial purposes. As for the Bennett New Deal, King had opposed much of it because he thought it both unconstitutional and costly. He therefore referred Bennett's legislation to the Supreme Court for an opinion. The problem of unemployment he assigned to the newly appointed National Employment Commission (NEC). Its chairman was a businessman of presumably sound views, Arthur Purvis.

King's attitude was understandable. It was also backward-looking. The Depression demonstrated that the division of tax fields and responsibilities made in 1867 was outdated. Suitable in an agricultural society, it had ceased to be appropriate even before the 1930s. The provinces did not have the resources to pay for unemployment relief. They needed help from the Dominion government, or they would have to default on their obligations.

Dunning nevertheless set out to create conditions under which the provinces would cease to look to Ottawa for loans and grants. He proposed a Provincial Loan Council, whose purpose was to restore the ability of the four western provinces to borrow in the open market. Ottawa would guarantee the bonds and the interest payable on them provided the Loan Council had approved them. Because the federal representative on the Council would have a veto power, Ottawa would effectively control the financial affairs of provinces that wished to borrow. Dunning and King believed that this would encourage greater provincial prudence in spending money, particularly on relief.

Several provinces rejected Dunning's proposal, none more vigorously than Alberta. William Aberhart's Social Credit government did not want outsiders to dictate its financial policies. Rather than knuckle under to Ottawa, Aberhart did the almost unthinkable. Alberta had a $3 million debenture due on April 1, 1936, but the government, lacking the money, simply refused to pay. It was the first default ever by a province of Canada.

The idea of a Provincial Loan Council quietly died. King and most of his cabinet were little disturbed by this, or by Alberta's default. Rather than continue making loans to the provinces, they were prepared to see Saskatchewan and Manitoba default as well. But Dunning disagreed. Ottawa would have to borrow in 1937 in order to repay maturing War Loans. If several provinces defaulted, the Dominion's credit rating would be affected and the government would have to pay higher interest rates. Reluctantly the cabinet decided to continue lending to the western provinces.

The continuing financial difficulties of these provinces prompted King to appoint the Royal Commission on Dominion-Provincial Relations. A further reason was the striking down in 1937 of most of the Bennett New Deal legislation. The Judicial Committee of the Privy Council ruled that several bills, including the Unemployment Insurance Act and the Natural Products Marketing Act, were unconstitutional. The Royal Commission's mandate was to enquire whether the division of responsibilities between the Dominion and the provinces still matched the division of tax resources.

While the Commission was doing its work, King had to fend off an unwelcome suggestion from Arthur Purvis's National Employment Commission. It recommended in 1938 that Ottawa assume full responsibility for unemployment relief. Other NEC proposals were no more welcome: that Ottawa establish a national network of labour exchanges, adopt a housing policy and a home improvement loan scheme, and expand facilities for vocational training of young people. All this would require money, which King was unwilling to spend. Purvis had not turned into a wild-eyed radical, however. His views were in line with those of clear-eyed businessmen. The Canadian Chamber of Commerce, for example, wanted Ottawa to assume responsibility for unemployment. The Depression had revealed grave problems in employment legislation and social services. Many businessmen realized that if capitalism were to recover to full health, such problems had to be solved.

King evidently cared less about these problems than he did about the financial health of his government, and more particularly about a balanced budget. Therefore he ignored the NEC's recommendations. The problems were under consideration by the Royal Commission on Dominion–Provincial Relations, he explained. When that Commission reported in 1940, it recommended that Ottawa take the steps necessary to introduce a nation-wide unemployment insurance scheme. With Canada now at war, and unemployment dropping rapidly, King's government

The first chairman of the Royal Commission on Dominion–Provincial Relations was N.W. Rowell, Chief Justice of Ontario. Later Joseph Sirois, a Laval University professor of law, succeeded him.

acted at last. Canada got a contributory unemployment scheme similar to the one the Bennett government had enacted in 1935.

Conclusion

While government and politics in the Depression years offer some evidence of a reformist spirit, there are, on the whole, more signs of political and social conservatism. Politicians assumed a greater importance than in the 1920s, but only a minority of them saw politics as a means to major change. Voters threw out governments mainly because they blamed them for unemployment or low prices. What they voted for, however, was not so much a turn to a radically different future as a return to a better past. It was unjustifiable but quite understandable that the 1920s came to resemble a lost economic golden age. Many Canadians hoped for nothing better than its revival.

This matched a general mood of conservatism, a hankering after the values of the past, though not necessarily those of the 1920s. The emancipation of women, for example, an accomplishment of the war and immediate postwar years, had left resentment in its wake. Advances in the workplace that women had made in the 1920s were often rolled back in the 1930s. In other ways conservatism persisted or asserted itself. Thus it continued to be illegal to spread information concerning birth control.

The 1930s showed little change in governmental practice. Not until late in the decade did some federal civil servants come to accept the idea that a budget deficit might stimulate the economy. Associated with the name of British economist John Maynard Keynes, this idea was that government spending should counteract spending in the private sector. If private industry was booming, government should seek to cool things down by raising taxes and running a budget surplus. If private industry was in a slump, as it was in the Depression, government should consciously plan for a budget deficit. This would give a boost to the economy. The long-range goal was to flatten out the economic highs and lows that came with business booms and busts. The short-range goals were to lessen unemployment and to break the pattern of deflation. Similar ideas influenced government policy in Sweden and the United States during the 1930s, but they had little effect in Canada. The deficits that Canadian governments experienced were unintended and in no way stimulative. They were the result of shortfalls in revenue that came about in spite of tax increases and reflected declines in business activity and employment. Canadian governments continued to strive for a balanced budget.

Yet there were positive accomplishments that outlasted the decade. Among these were the advent of public broadcasting, a national airline company, and the Bank of Canada. The Canadian Broadcasting Corporation took shape in the mid-thirties.

Trans Canada Airlines, the forerunner of Air Canada, made its first flight in 1937. The Bank of Canada, formed in 1934 as a privately owned central bank, was the first agency enabling effective control of monetary policy. (After taking office in 1935 the Liberals made the bank publicly owned.) There were also important innovations in agriculture, and some modest political accomplishments at the provincial level. Nevertheless, the scene in government and politics changed relatively little in the 1930s. Only after war came in September 1939 did the rate of change accelerate.

REVIEW AND DISCUSSION

Key People and Ideas
Explain the importance of each of the following as they are discussed in the chapter.

W.L. Mackenzie King
Richard Bedford Bennett
James Shaver Woodsworth
W.D. Herridge
Harry H. Stevens
Agnes Macphail
John Bracken
Tomas Dufferin Pattullo
William Aberhart
Mitchell Hepburn
L.-A. Taschereau

Lionel Groulx
Maurice Duplessis
The CCF
The Regina Manifesto
Social Credit
The Royal Commission
    on Dominion–Provincial
    Relations
Union nationale
The Padlock Act
National Employment
    Commission

Analysing the Issues
Answer each of the following questions, which deal with important issues raised in the chapter.

1. What factors led to the Conservative victory in 1930?

2. What arguments convinced R.B. Bennett that Canadians needed a "New Deal" in 1935?
3. What new political parties were formed in Canada during the 1930s?
4. What were the major conflicts between the federal and provincial governments during the 1930s?

Questions for Discussion
Think carefully about the following question and discuss the issues it raises.
1. Several new political parties were formed in Canada during the 1930s. The governing party lost the federal elections of both 1930 and 1935. Also, most provincial governments were defeated in elections during the 1930s. What factors do you think accounted for this mood of change in Canadian politics during the 1930s? On balance, do you think Canadians were well served by the new governments they elected during the decade? Use evidence from the chapter to justify your point of view.

6

HOW CANADIANS
WORKED AND LIVED

Thirty years after the Depression ended, John David Eaton, of the department store Eatons, spoke to a reporter about the 1930s. They were a time he remembered with affection. "Nobody thought about money in those days because they never saw any. You could take your girl to a supper dance at the hotel for $10, and that included the bottle and a room for you and your friends to drink it in. I'm glad I grew up then. It was a good time for everybody. People learned what it means to work."

Eaton's inherited wealth made it easy for him to look at the bright side. In general the Depression years were better than tolerable for that minority of Canadians who had a secure job and income. Frank Underhill, a professor of history at the University of Toronto during the 1930s, later recalled: "I wasn't angry because I didn't suffer much. I was a full professor; for the first and only time in my life I belonged to a small social group who enjoyed a superior status, economic and social." Professors were unlikely to lose their job. Their income was not large, but it was secure.

Even those who were unemployed do not necessarily remember the Depression as a completely miserable time. Hugh Garner, a newspaperman and novelist who was a hobo during much of the 1930s, later wrote:

> The Depression was tough, but it wasn't all hunger and sadness. There were picnics, corn roasts and cheap dances . . . . Young people fell in love and married. After all, a married relief cheque was better than two single people getting nothing at all . . . . Babies were born, whether their fathers were unemployed or not, and their young mothers made do with handmade or hand-me-down layettes. A wicker laundry basket is just as good a bassinet as a store-bought one. Do you want to know something? I don't think I'd have wanted to miss the Great Depression for the world.

Another newspaperman, Dennis Braithwaite, told his readers in the late 1960s that a depression was really nothing much to worry about. Life in the 1930s was simpler; people learned to make do with less. "In a depression steaks are hard to come by, and round steak is about the best you can hope for. So people are forced to get by on such cruel fare as home-made vegetable soup, home-made beans with molasses, rice pudding with raisins, pot roast with pan-baked potatoes and roasted onions, chickens fried, boiled or roasted, home-made preserves and pickles—all that terrible stuff."

This makes the Dirty Thirties seem almost like good fun. We need to be cautious in interpreting such stories, however. People who recall the period of their youth often see it through rose-coloured glasses. Memories are usually mellowed by the passage of time. Things that were enjoyable or exciting are remembered more readily than those that were unpleasant. This does not mean that what our parents and grandparents remember is not true. It

Opposite page: Vancouver strikers march past a theatre showing the hit comedy of 1938, *You Can't Take it With You.*

does mean that the truth has been filtered. To know what life was like during the Depression, we must do more than talk to those who remember it.

Canadians at Work

Even at the worst point of the Depression approximately three-quarters of the Canadian work force was employed. However, many of them were insecure and poor. They might be laid off; their jobs might disappear. Wages, seldom generous to begin with, had been cut and cut again. Canadians who were materially comfortable were in the minority.

In 1940, Leonard Marsh published a study of social classes in Canada, *Canadians In and Out of Work*. Using 1931 census data he divided Canadian families into the following categories:

	Number of Families	Percentage
Well-to-do	12 500	0.6
Middle classes	504 000	25.1
Working classes	862 000	42.8
Farm classes	633 700	31.5
	2 012 200	100.0

The well-to-do were those with annual family incomes above $10 000. The heads of these families were prominent in finance, industry and the independent professions. A handful of them were leading public servants. Some 2000 families enjoyed incomes of more than $10 000 solely from investments. By the standards of the time, that made them rich indeed. Only 600–700 families had incomes in excess of $50 000 a year.

The middle classes included several groups—small businessmen, professional, technical, managerial and commercial workers, and "responsible and independent industrial workers," such as foremen and skilled artisans. In 1931 annual family income in these groups ranged from $1500 to $10 000. Middle-class workers typically received an annual salary rather than an hourly wage. This conferred a definite social status, as did having a "clean" job and wearing a white rather than a blue collar to work. Below a family income of $2500 a year, however, it would have been difficult to maintain a middle-class style of life.

Middle-class families commonly lived in houses that they owned rather than rented, although they were likely to have a mortgage. They generally owned a car, a radio, and various appliances, and they almost certainly had a telephone. Their children tended to complete high school, but only a minority of them went on to university. Because domestic servants were plentiful during

Hats varied in shape and size, but no fashionable woman considered herself well dressed without one.

the Depression—room, board and $8 to $10 a month were common terms—many of the better-off families had one, usually a young woman.

In descending order of income and status the working, or wage-earning classes were skilled, semi-skilled and unskilled. These last were almost one fifth of the Canadian male work force. Many of them were recent immigrants. Wages were low and the rate of unemployment was high.

The working classes totalled just over two-fifths of all Canadian families. If we include the low-income segments of the middle and farming classes with the working class, however, it comprised more than half of all family units. Married women in this group quite often worked outside the home in order to add to family income, and children were taken out of school as soon as possible and sent out to work. After paying for food, shelter and clothing, there was little left over for the comforts of life or for savings, to say nothing of luxuries. Working-class people generally rented their homes, and if some of them owned cars they were usually second hand.

In the farming classes were owners, tenant farmers and farm labourers. Some owners were well-to-do, others were miserably poor. Many got by, but not with ease. Tenant farmers were likely to be badly off, farm labourers almost certain to be so.

Because of their relative isolation, farmers were more likely than city folk to have bought cars during the 1920s. One in six farm families had a radio, generally battery-operated as only ten percent of all farms had electricity in 1931. Running water in the kitchen was scarcely more common, and only one in twenty farms had running water in a bathroom. The outhouse had largely disappeared from Canadian cities and towns, but in the country almost every family still had one.

Poverty

What proportion of Canadians were poor during the 1930s? An answer is hard to come by. It was (and is) difficult to set agreed-upon tests of poverty which apply equally to city dwellers and farmers, to single people and families.

It seems likely that about one-half of Canadian families were, in the early 1930s, poor by any definition. If a working-class family managed to avoid the most grinding poverty, it was often because there were two or more income earners. Women and young people just out of school earned considerably less than did adult men. Women, for example, typically earned about half of what men did for comparable work. But that amount was usually enough to keep the wolf from the door, provided there was a chief breadwinner who had not lost his job.

When unemployment lasted for any length of time it had a

devastating effect on working-class families. So did loss of income due to illness or old age. Few working-class families belonged to private insurance schemes or pension plans, and few had more than the most meagre savings. Mostly people worked as long as they could and hoped that their children would then be able to support them. This was common in rural Canada. When children had moved to the city, leaving their parents behind, the matter became more difficult. The houses that working-class city dwellers could afford to rent or buy were generally too small to accommodate aging parents.

By 1930 Ontario and the four western provinces had introduced or announced non-contributory old age pensions in response to a federal promise to pay half the cost of such provincial schemes. Men and women 70 years of age or over, who were British subjects and had lived in Canada for at least 20 years, were eligible. Means tests made it hard to qualify, however: potential recipients had to show that they really needed the pension of up to $20 per month. The *Toronto Star* charged in October 1929 that the Ontario government scheme would cover only 20 000 of the 120 000 Ontarians aged 70 and over.

The three Atlantic provinces introduced old age pensions in 1931 after Prime Minister R.B. Bennett raised the federal share of the cost to three-quarters. However, Quebec did not have old age pensions until 1936. Small wonder that there are occasional stories in newspapers in the early thirties about old people sleeping outside even in winter. "Such old people present a problem which it seems impossible to solve," a coroner said, commenting on the situation of an old man who had frozen to death. "Without friends or relatives, no one assumes responsibility for them, so that often they have to be committed to jail for want of another place to send them."

Ill health, even when it did not lead to unemployment, was a serious threat to the poor. Those who were on relief got a basic minimum of health care free of charge. Those who worked, however, were expected to pay their own medical and dental bills. The working poor, therefore, saw a physician only in extreme cases, and might then be unable to pay his bill. (In the 1930s the great majority of doctors and dentists were men.) Most practitioners carried a certain number of patients as charity cases. That number grew during the Depression, when it became hard even for many doctors and dentists to make ends meet.

Among the letters that R.B. Bennett received while he was prime minister were many that asked for financial help with medical problems. A woman in rural Quebec who was going blind asked for money to see an ophthalmologist. A young man from Alberta asked for money to buy a new artificial leg. From Nova Scotia a man wrote that his daughter had tonsillitis: "The doctor called and told me that she must have the tonsils out . . . . Now I cannot have it done unless I get help from some source to do it. In January I had a sick spell that cost $100. I am trying to pay that and now here is $40 more. Would you please assist in this?''

M.J. Coldwell, the leader of the Saskatchewan Farmer–Labour Party in the early 1930s, later recalled that while he was campaigning in 1934 a farmer approached him after his speech and said: "I'm going to vote for you because the capitalist system killed my daughter." He told how, when his daughter got a bad stomach-ache, he had taken her to the nearest physician, who had examined her free of charge. An immediate operation was necessary, the doctor said, but although he would operate without charging a fee, the hospital required $10 cash. It took the farmer a couple of days to borrow this sum, in dribs and drabs, from various neighbours, and by the time he got his daughter to the hospital it was too late. The doctor operated immediately, but the child died. Her appendix had burst and peritonitis, an infection that was almost always fatal before the discovery of antibiotics, had set in. How many similar tales could be told, in those days before state-funded medical care, by people who had no money and were too proud to beg for charity?

M.J. Coldwell later replaced J.S. Woodsworth as national leader of the CCF, a position he held for two decades.

Making Do

Growing numbers of working-class Canadians faced unemployment and destitution in the early 1930s. Those who continued to work, whether they were working or middle class, usually saw their incomes drop. Because of lower consumer prices, however, those who continued working often had an increasing real income.

Unable to pay the rent, a Montreal family is turned out onto the street.

Real Income
Consumer prices fell by 23
percent from 1929 to 1933.
An income of $770 in
1933, therefore, was the
same in real terms as a
$1000 income in 1929, that
is it would, on average,
buy the same package of
goods and services.
Someone who earned $900
in 1933 would have a real
income that was 17 percent
higher than the $1000 he
earned in 1929.

A package of 20 cigarettes
cost 25 cents, a bottle of
whisky $2 or more. In real
terms, taking into account
increases in prices and
incomes since then,
tobacco products and
alcoholic beverages were
considerably more
expensive back in the
1930s.

Marriage and Birth Rates
The marriage rate fell from
7.7 per 1000 population in
1929 to 5.9 in 1932 and
stayed below the 1929 rate
until 1937. The birth rate
fell from 23.9 per 1000
population in 1930 to a
low point of 20.1 in 1937
before it began to rise
again.

If you were lucky enough to have a steady job with an income of, say, $2400 a year, you could make do very nicely. Prices dropped to levels that had not been seen for more than 15 years. In 1932 in Toronto a 6-bottle carton of Coca Cola was advertised at 27 cents. Butter was 18 cents a pound, so was prime rib roast. Apples were 29 cents a dozen. A small detached bungalow rented for $15 a month; houses could be bought for as little as $2000.

The 1930s were not years devoid of opportunity. Through hard work, shrewdness and good luck some people prospered. In 1930, for instance, W.A.C. Bennett, aged 29, bought a hardware store in Kelowna, B.C. In 1931 Roy Thomson, then 36, opened a radio station in North Bay, Ontario. Neither Bennett, later to be premier of British Columbia, nor Thomson, who died in 1976 as Lord Thomson of Fleet, found the early going easy. Both eventually saw their enterprises flourish.

Few people, however, had the money to take advantage of the bargains or the opportunities. They learned to do without pleasures that cost money. Cigarettes and alcoholic beverages were relatively expensive, so most people smoked and drank little. Most generally managed to enjoy themselves all the same. However, there were increases in the number of illegitimate births, cases of mental illness, suicide and attempted suicide. Observers took these to be evidence of the economic distress of the 1930s. Tuberculosis also increased, the result of malnutrition and overcrowding.

Population and Migration

According to the census of 1931, Canada's population was 10 376 786. Ten years later it was 11 506 655. This was an increase of 10.9 percent for the decade. Never in Canadian history has the rate of increase between census dates been lower. Canadians postponed marriage and had fewer children than in the 1920s, and not surprisingly, the rate of natural increase (live births minus deaths) slowed. Nevertheless, had it not been for natural increase the population of Canada would actually have fallen. Since the beginning of the twentieth century, immigration had made an important contribution to population growth. Between the 1931 and 1941 censuses, however, 92 000 more people left Canada than came in.

There was little immigration in the 1930s as the Canadian government deliberately restricted it in order to protect the job market for existing residents. In 1935, for example, only 11 277 immigrants entered.

Prejudice as well as concern about unemployment played a part in reducing immigration. Large numbers had come in during the later 1920s, many of them from central and eastern Europe, the so-called (at the time) "non-preferred countries." Their presence sat badly with many Canadians of British and French stock. An Anglican bishop, George Exton Lloyd, claimed in 1928 that the Canadian people were in danger of being "mongrelized."

In 1929 the Mackenzie King government reduced the number of immigrants allowed in, though not by enough according to the Conservatives, who campaigned on the issue in 1930. Some argued that a large number of unemployables had come to Canada; others worried that a growing number of unemployed central European workers were a threat to social order.

The hostility to recent immigrants grew as the Depression deepened. Some believed that they were getting preferential treatment and complained bitterly to Prime Minister Bennett. Labour leaders claimed that Canadian-born workers had to "stand around and starve" while foreigners got jobs, allegedly because they were willing to work for less.

In fact, recent immigrants suffered more from unemployment than those who had been in the country longer or had been born in Canada. As well, communities often refused relief to unemployed foreigners, many of whom became transients, riding the rails in search for work. What they mostly found was discrimination.

In 1929 and 1930 the governments of Alberta and Saskatchewan refused to accept several thousand Mennonite refugees, farmers from the Soviet Union. This refusal had widespread public support in those provinces, even though the Soviet government said that it would send the Mennonites to Siberian labour camps if no country would admit them. Later in the decade the Canadian government showed great unwillingness to admit Jewish refugees from Nazi Germany. Hitler's rise to power in 1933 led to increasing persecution of German Jews. Repression also hit other groups, notably gypsies and opponents of the Nazi regime. A growing number of people sought to escape Germany, and that number grew after Germany annexed Austria in 1938.

Some 600 of these Mennonites managed to escape into China, and later went to the United States and Paraguay. The remainder were mostly sent into Siberian exile. Many of them died there.

Canadian policy was to admit political refugees only in very exceptional circumstances. Those who had money and wished to farm might be accepted; others were not welcome. Few of the refugees were wealthy, however, and few were farmers. The government's primary concern was to safeguard jobs for those who already lived in Canada. Added to this, however, was a racism that in this case directed itself against central and eastern Europeans in general, and Jews in particular. A left-wing periodical, *The Canadian Forum,* noted in March 1939:

> The arguments against admitting refugees are mostly economic, but racial and national prejudice, though less vocal, is probably the most powerful factor. It seems to us less important to preserve the preponderance of British (or French) blood, than to preserve the spirit of liberty and democracy . . . . Racial exclusiveness is no less stupid in Canada than it is in Germany.

Within the cabinet and civil service, however, a different view prevailed: refugees, particularly Jewish refugees, were not wanted. Insofar as there was a public opinion on this issue, it also ran against admitting refugees. Only a very few managed to enter Canada.

At the same time as immigration was being restricted, tens of thousands of Canadian residents were heading for the apparently greener pastures of the United States. Thousands more returned to the British Isles and continental Europe. Some of them went voluntarily, having become convinced that the New World had less to offer them than the old. Others were deported. The grounds for deportation included becoming a charge on the public or being arrested for vagrancy, as well as expressing opinions that the government deemed to be unacceptably radical. Concern about the threat of communism led in the early 1930s to the deportation of dozens of Communist party members who had been active as political propagandists or labour organizers.

The 1931 census identified 53.7 percent of the population as urban; in 1941, even after almost two years of war that greatly increased urban employment, the figure was only 54.3.

There was a good deal of internal migration. Not surprisingly, the three prairie provinces lost many people. The population of Saskatchewan fell by 26 000 from 1931 to 1941—natural increase could not make up for those who pulled up stakes and left. When they did not leave Canada altogether, they went mainly to Ontario and British Columbia.

The movement from rural to urban Canada, which had begun late in the nineteenth century, came close to stalling. Canadians who lived on the farms and in the villages of central Canada and the Atlantic provinces by and large stayed there.

Labour Organization

There was no unified movement of protest against unemployment and falling wages. People might complain, as a Montrealer did about the miserably low salaries paid to bank clerks: $8.50 a week, he said, was simply not enough to marry and establish a family. However, such complaints did not lead to united action.

Craft Unions
Craft unions were organized on the basis of a particular skill or craft, such as typography, cabinet making or plumbing.

What protest there was expressed itself most dramatically in strikes and labour organization. In the early 1930s several bitter strikes ensued when companies tried to impose major wage cuts. Unions associated with the Trades and Labour Congress (TLC) had some success in maintaining themselves. In any case, wage rates in unionized industries fell far less rapidly than did those in non-unionized industries.

The TLC was a conservative group. It was made up of craft unions and was affiliated with the equally conservative American Federation of Labour. The TLC showed very little interest in organizing the non-unionized majority of Canadian workers. The members of its union affiliates saw themselves as the "aristocracy" of labour. They were more concerned with maintaining the relatively high wage rates of the skilled trades than with raising the wages of semi-skilled or unskilled workers.

Other, more radical groups took up the challenge. Foremost among them were the Workers' Unity League (WUL) and the Unemployed Workers Association. Both were Communist-led. They faced hostility from employers, the TLC, and governments at all levels. WUL organizers were liable to be arrested and charged with vagrancy or even sedition; during the early 1930s their efforts often led to jail sentences and even deportation.

Industrial Unions
Industrial unions were organized on the basis of an entire industry, such as automobiles, steel or mining.

The WUL was active in organizing semi-skilled and unskilled workers into industrial unions. In spite of several major strikes, its successes were few. Its defeats were often bloody. A 1931 strike by the Mine Workers Union of Canada, a WUL affiliate, in Bienfait, Saskatchewan, led to a demonstration in nearby Estevan protesting the company's use of strike breakers. The demonstration defied a ban on parades through the town, violence broke out, and the police shot and killed three strikers. Twenty-two others were arrested, and the strike collapsed. A coal mining strike in Corbin, British Columbia, four years later also led to violence: a fight between strikers and police left 16 policemen and 25 strikers injured, some seriously.

In Stratford, Ontario, the Chesterfield and Furniture Workers Union, another WUL affiliate, led its members out on strike in September 1933. The unrest spread to the local meat-processing plant and resulted in a strike by the women who worked there plucking chickens for two cents a bird. When tempers grew hot, the mayor and police commission asked the provincial government for help in keeping the peace. This prompted the dispatch of regular soldiers, two companies of the Royal Canadian Regiment and four machine gun carriers, from London and Toronto. The government's heavy-handed action won the strikers considerable sympathy, but in the end the strikes gained them little else.

In 1935, the Communist party's interests had shifted to the international scene and it decided to end the WUL's activities. Labour unrest nonetheless continued to grow. In the period of economic recovery, particularly during 1936 and 1937, workers had more leverage than they had had earlier. At first there was little effective leadership, but by late 1936, unions affiliated with the Committee for Industrial Organization (CIO), a new American labour group, were catching the attention of Canadian workers. Steel workers, auto workers, electrical workers and others wanted company recognition of their new unions as well as increased job security, higher wages and improved working conditions. Occasionally using the "sitdown strike" to dramatize their protest against their employers, American workers inspired their Canadian cousins, some of whom invited the CIO north.

The most important of the strikes resulting from CIO activity

The 1933 strike in Stratford, Ontario, was the last time in Canadian history that troops were used to maintain order during an industrial dispute.

took place against General Motors of Canada. Early in 1937, the company announced its fifth pay cut in a row and posted a more demanding production schedule. As the American parent company had just announced record profits, the Canadian workers were very unhappy. They listened eagerly to men like Charlie Millard, a fellow worker and former small businessman who had been ruined by the Depression. Millard led an Oshawa local of the United Auto Workers (UAW). Assisted by an organizer from Detroit, the UAW had little difficulty in signing up most of General Motors' 4000 employees in Oshawa. Negotiations between the union and the company then began, but they broke down when Premier Mitchell Hepburn intervened. He feared that a UAW success would encourage other CIO-affiliated unions to try to organize workers in the gold mines of northern Ontario. This he opposed on both economic and personal grounds: he had good friends among the mine owners, and occasionally speculated in the shares of mining companies himself. He therefore encouraged General Motors management to resist union demands.

A strike was called in April 1937. In spite of Hepburn's continued efforts to prevent a settlement, the UAW managed to secure, for all practical purposes, the company's recognition of its status as bargaining agent for the Oshawa plant's workers. Other strikes by CIO unions had less success, however. The economy worsened later in 1937, and this undermined organizing drives as well as the willingness of workers to go out on strike. At the same time it reinforced the resolve of companies to resist unionization.

A Middle-Class Country

One key difficulty that union organizers faced in the 1930s was that most Canadians, including many working-class people, looked on unions with suspicion, even hostility. They seemed to be institutions alien to a country of immigrants, of people who had come to improve their own economic position, preferably to work for themselves rather than someone else. Working-class consciousness was not high. Indeed, observers judged Canada as a whole to have a middle-class atmosphere.

There were several reasons for this. The middle classes were concentrated in the towns and cities and were therefore more visible than their proportion in the population, approximately 25 percent, would have suggested. At the same time they were far more numerous than the wealthy. Virtues admired by the middle class— hard work, honesty, cleanliness, sobriety, prudence—dominated newspapers, magazines and radio programmes. The advertising that they carried reflected middle-class living standards. The major social institutions reflected middle-class influences and values. Churches, schools and service organizations offered many examples of this. The people employed in them came from the middle class or considered themselves to be middle class.

Churches

The churches assumed great importance as social centres and agents of charity as well as places of worship. Approximately three out of five Canadians identified themselves as Protestant: most belonged to the recently formed (1925) United Church of Canada or to the Anglican, Baptist, Presbyterian, Lutheran or Mennonite churches. Almost all remaining Canadians were Roman Catholic. Jews made up about one percent of the population; Muslims and others were fewer still. In 1931 only 21 155 Canadians stated that they had no religion.

To the middle-class virtues identified earlier the churches added charity and piety. On the whole, they were bastions of respectability and did not challenge the existing social and economic conditions. The emphasis was on conventional charity, giving to the less fortunate. Congregations in central Canada were particularly active in sending food and clothing to the prairie provinces.

A more radical view of the church's responsibility had some influence in the United Church of Canada. This was in part a continuation of the Social Gospel that had been influential in the Methodist Church earlier in the century. Methodists made up the larger part of the United Church, and among its ministers there were scores who came to see the Depression as proof that the capitalist system was un-Christian. Their alternative was a Christian type of socialism, and they formed the Fellowship for a Christian Social Order to promote their goals. These went much too far for

The United Church
The United Church of Canada was a fusion of the Methodists, Congregationalists and a majority of Presbyterians. Approximately one-third of the Presbyterians refused to join and maintained their separate church.

most United Church people, however. Some sought the reform of capitalism, rather than its overthrow, but the large majority of laymen—and a lot of ministers as well—thought it improper for the church to involve itself too much in politics and economics.

Many congregations experienced great hardship during the Depression. When the incomes of members dropped, church income declined as well. This made it hard to pay ministers, maintain church buildings and carry on church work. Sometimes congregations had no choice but to appeal to outside help. In 1932 the members of a congregation in Stittsville, just west of Ottawa, explained to R.B. Bennett that the wheels of the funeral lorry had broken through the floor. "We find ourselves up against it as our congregation is only 30 families and practically all farmers." They hoped that Bennett would make a contribution towards a new floor. He sent five dollars.

Education

For the schools and universities of Canada, as for the churches, the Depression posed difficult challenges. As income from property taxes fell, school boards found it ever harder to make ends meet. They cut down on everything: books and supplies, maintenance, teachers' salaries. In hard-hit Saskatchewan, the annual salaries of rural teachers dropped from $1076 in 1930 to a mere $476 five years later. In much of Canada salaries were little better.

In many poor school districts teachers did not get paid in cash at all. They got a place to live, food and fuel, and the school board's promise that they would get paid whenever it might have money. Novelist Max Braithwaite took a one-room school in Saskatchewan in 1933. The salary was $450 a year, payable in ten monthly installments. Of this $250 was in kind. "So you'll have another twenty a month coming," the school board chairman said, as reported in Braithwaite's book *Don't Shoot the Teacher*. Any hope the young teacher had of buying a new suit was soon dashed, however: "We can't give you any cash. We just haven't got any. You'll have to take a promissory note, and I'm damned if I know when we'll be able to make it good." Since Braithwaite did not have the money for the train ride back to Saskatoon, he had little choice. He took the job but he felt a lasting anger, one shared by many teachers in the 1930s.

The construction of schools came to a virtual halt. Existing buildings became increasingly crowded as young people tended to stay in school longer. What was the point of leaving early if one could not get a job? Nevertheless, in 1933 only two out of three pupils completed the first eight grades, and only one in five graduated from high school. The upper grades continued to serve mainly a relatively small social elite.

Canadian universities were even more elitist. Total full-time

Social Service Council of Canada
Several Protestant denominations co-operated in the Social Service Council of Canada, which had some success in getting industrial reforms adopted. For example, a report by Rev. C.W. Gordon on the Canadian steel industry led to a reduction of daily hours of work in the Sydney, Nova Scotia, steel mills from 13 to 11.

Teachers' Salaries
Among the best paid were the teachers of Toronto, who in 1932–33 averaged $2200. The range was from $4625 to $650, however, and while men tended to be in the top half of this range, most women teachers were in the bottom half. Even so, they often provided bits of food to pupils whose families were even worse off.

enrolment in 1930 was 32 926; in 1935 it was 35 108. Women were considerably less likely to attend university than men. Many parents still regarded higher education for women as a frill. When money was tight, families might still send their son to college, but not their daughter. And for many families, and their university-age children, money during the Depression was tight indeed.

Nevertheless, enrolment grew steadily during the 1930s, probably because, then as now, it was easier to get a job with a university degree than with a high school diploma. However, even with a degree there were few sure jobs. Max Braithwaite recalls that in 1933 in Saskatchewan "it was said—and I believe it—that of the entire graduating class of engineers that year one man got a job. And that was a job driving a truck."

Two further developments in education should be noted. The first was the growth of adult education. The Canadian Association for Adult Education was founded in 1934, and by 1936 there were experiments in the use of radio for educational extension work in both Alberta and British Columbia. The other development was the increasing influence of "progressive" education, that is, education centring on the child who was learning rather than on the subject matter being taught. This movement originated in the United States and spread into primary schools throughout Canada.

University Enrolment In 1975, when the population of Canada was just over twice the size of 1935, total fulltime enrolment in universities was 371 000, more than ten times the number in 1935.

Radio Broadcasting

One aspect of the interwar years was the growing number and importance of national volunteer organizations. Among those founded during those years were the Canadian Teachers' Federation, the Canadian Institute of International Affairs, the Canadian Federation of University Women's Clubs, the Canadian Authors' Association, and the Canadian Radio League. All these groups helped to stimulate the growth of a national self-awareness. Perhaps none did more than the Canadian Radio League.

The Radio League was founded in 1930 by two energetic young men, Alan Plaunt and Graham Spry. Its primary purpose was to persuade the Dominion government to implement the recommendations of the Royal Commission on Radio Broadcasting. The Aird Commission, named after its chairman, the Toronto banker Sir John Aird, had concluded that the interests of Canada and Canadian radio listeners could "be adequately served only by some form of public ownership, operation and control behind which is the national power and prestige of the whole public of the Dominion of Canada."

Plaunt was independently wealthy and willing to use some of his money to finance the cause. As national secretary of the Association of Canadian Clubs, Spry had contacts across the country, and he used them to marshall support for public broadcasting.

The Radio League's chief argument was that private broadcasting, if unregulated, would be increasingly controlled by American business interests. It would be Americanized, commercialized and shallow.

There was in fact evidence that commercial broadcasting was hampering the expression of Canadian views and the use of Canadian talent. The radio fare available in the early 1930s was mostly light entertainment, it was American, and it was increasingly "network" radio. Its purpose was to deliver ever larger numbers of North American listeners to advertisers, and in this it was succeeding. To those who wanted to use radio as an agency of education or high culture, however, or as a means of drawing Canadians closer together, commercial radio was a failure.

A court decision in 1932 held that radio broadcasting was within the federal government's jurisdiction. Pressured by the Radio League, the Bennett government created the three-member Canadian Radio Broadcasting Commission (CRBC) in 1932. It was to control and regulate private broadcasting in Canada and to carry on the business of broadcasting itself. Its autonomy and finances were both too limited to carry out these heavy responsibilities, however, and its performance struck observers, including Spry, as less than satisfactory. In 1936 the King government replaced it with the Canadian Broadcasting Corporation (CBC), which had more ample powers and performed reasonably well during the next few years.

The first thing most school children did when they got home was tune in for the adventures of the Lone Ranger.

Sports and Entertainment

One popular programme that the CBC carried from coast to coast was "Hockey Night in Canada." This Saturday night feature made Foster Hewitt's voice familiar to hundreds of thousands of Canadians and demonstrated how great an interest there was in spectator sport. Of course, sports also felt the impact of the Depression. National Hockey League franchises in Ottawa, Philadelphia and Pittsburgh folded in the early 1930s. Most of the remaining clubs were losing money, and in 1932 the NHL had to limit the teams' salaries and number of players. The individual salary ceiling was cut to $7500 per year, and each club was limited to a total salary bill of $70 000 for the 14 players it was allowed to carry.

Canadian professional football was run along even more frugal lines. The first western team to win the Grey Cup, the 1935 Winnipeg Blue Bombers, had a total salary budget of only $7500. The victory gave a great boost to football in the West, but eastern teams complained about the eight American players the Blue Bombers had used. A new residency requirement for players kept the 1936 western champions, the Regina Rough Riders, from competing for the Grey Cup. Thus began an era of bad east–west feelings among football clubs and fans that did not come to an end until after the Second World War.

The most successful Canadian team in any sport during the 1930s (and probably of all time) was the Edmonton Commercial Graduates. They dominated women's basketball for almost 20 years before disbanding in 1940. Although women's basketball was not yet an Olympic sport, the Grads swept tournaments held at the same time as four consecutive Olympic Games, including those at Los Angeles in 1932 and Berlin in 1936.

For fans and players, professional and amateur sports were a welcome escape from the worries of the Depression years. Shinny on a frozen field in winter, sandlot baseball or box lacrosse in the spring and summer, football in the fall: interest in all of these was high. Soccer, rugby, horse racing, cycling, swimming, and track and field were also popular. The equipment might be battered, the uniforms old, but the enthusiasm did not suffer.

Going to the movies was another popular diversion, although ticket prices of 25 to 50 cents were a lot of money to the poor. Most of the films as well as their stars were American. There was a small Canadian feature film industry in the 1930s, but it found the competition from the United States too stiff. Canadian actors like Raymond Massey, Mary Pickford and Walter Pidgeon made their mark outside Canada.

The 1930s, the first full decade of the "talkies," were in many ways the golden age of the cinema. Fine directors were at work, making films that were witty, thrilling, funny, deeply serious—and that managed to please large audiences. Mostly they were made in black and white, though colour came into use during the 1930s.

One of the top Hollywood stars of the thirties, Winnipeg-born Deanna Durban was proudly claimed as Canada's own.

Perhaps the most memorable Depression movie was *The Grapes of Wrath,* directed by John Ford. Released in 1940, it was based on John Steinbeck's novel about a family of "Okies," sharecroppers from dried-out Oklahoma, who trekked to California in search of a new life. Henry Fonda's portrayal of the young farmer, Tom Joad, hopeful yet sombre, seemed to capture the essence of the Dirty Thirties. Most viewers preferred escape over social documentaries, however. More than any other genres, comedies and the musicals of Busby Berkeley typified the decade. Yet the comedies were rarely completely mindless. The reality of the Depression was often present. Many viewers must have winced when they heard William Powell, the debonair star of the very funny *My Man Godfrey,* say: "The only difference between a derelict and a man is a job."

In that age before television, the newsreels which preceded the feature films were very important. They acquainted ordinary people with places and events far removed from their experience. After May 1934, one of the recurring images on the screen was that of the Dionne quintuplets. Born to a French-Canadian couple near Callander in northern Ontario, the quints and their physi-

TO OUR FIRST LOVE
Karo

THE DIONNES

cian, Dr. A.R. Dafoe, became a focus of international attention. The odds against identical quintuplets being conceived were astronomically high, even higher against their being born and higher yet against all five surviving. But survive they did. Raised under the protection of the Ontario government, apart from their parents, Annette, Cécile, Emilie, Marie and Yvonne were for years a major tourist attraction.

Periodicals, the Arts and Scholarship

Movie newsreels and radio newscasts were still relatively new ways of learning what was going on in the world. Newspapers retained much of their importance and influence. People read them for the news stories and editorials, for the classified ads, and for the popular features and comic strips. Not that newspapers had an easy time of it: advertising revenue lagged and profits fell. Although the population of Canada rose by 8 percent from 1931 to 1939, newspaper circulation went up very little. Two trends that had been evident earlier continued: the number of daily and weekly newspapers declined, and newspaper chains grew.

The 1930s were a difficult time for magazines as well. Popular weeklies like *Maclean's* and *Saturday Night* suffered losses in advertising revenue. They also had to face stiff competition from glossy American imports, among them *Collier's,* the *Saturday Evening Post* and a newcomer, *Time. The Canadian Forum,* a small monthly concerned with public affairs and the arts, almost went under in 1936. It was ultimately kept alive only by financial contributions from its readers.

Literature and the arts generally fared badly. During the Depression even established novelists like Morley Callaghan and Frederick Philip Grove found it hard to get their books published. Poets had an even more difficult time. Publishing houses retrenched and cut down on their lists. Some went broke as Canadians bought fewer books.

The Depression changed the direction of writing. Dramatists as well as novelists and poets became more critically aware of their society. Among the poets, A.M. Klein, Dorothy Livesay, Leo Kennedy and F.R. Scott attacked the economic system. Anne Marriott's "The Wind Our Enemy" offered an unsentimental depiction of the drought-stricken prairies. Morley Callaghan's novel *They Shall Inherit the Earth* and Claudius Gregory's *Forgotten Men* came to grips with the effects of unemployment, but no novel did so better than Irene Baird's *Waste Heritage,* a gripping fictional account of the 1938 On-to-Victoria trek.

Professional drama also suffered from the financial retrenchment of the Depression years. Some actors and directors got work with the new CBC, adapting drama to radio. Already in the 1920s, however, many theatres that had been used by touring companies

Opposite page:
Images of the thirties.

were being converted into movie houses or torn down. Canada had no secure tradition of theatre attendance; during the interwar years most people who had money to spend came to prefer the movies to live theatre. The other performing arts also offered few opportunities to professionals. Music and dance had always been badly funded, and live music performances were experiencing a serious challenge from phonograph records and radio. Juke boxes, playing popular records for a nickel, became common in cafés and drugstores. Although professional performers had a hard time, however, amateurs flourished. This was particularly true in drama. Amateur music and drama offered great scope for local participation, and admission was free or very cheap. These were powerful advantages. The launching of the Dominion Drama Festival in 1932 signaled the growing interest in "little theatre." The first Canada-wide finals took place the following year.

Professional painters and sculptors had a very difficult time. Public patronage for works of art, never large in Canada, virtually dried up. The budget of the National Gallery of Canada in Ottawa was $130 000 in 1929; it fell to $25 000 in 1934. From 1932 to 1936 the Gallery bought only two contemporary Canadian works. Nor did private collectors spend much, and when they did buy they preferred works by artists whose reputations were already safely established, such as the Group of Seven. Still, for most artists life in the 1920s had not been all that much easier. As painter David Milne said, "Artists stand depressions quite well; depressions look so much like their regular brand of prosperity."

There was no public support for scholarship, so it was hard for scholars to do research, and harder still to get even the most worthy scholarly works into print. Especially in the humanities, in fields like literary criticism and philosophy, not much was happening. Publishers were doing little; libraries were buying little. Indeed, libraries were generally just as badly off as the people who borrowed their books or visited their reading rooms simply to stay warm.

Conclusion

To live in Depression Canada was in many ways dispiriting. The 1930s exposed many Canadians to unusual hardship and made them well-acquainted with disappointment. They worked when they had the opportunity, however, and lived their lives as best they could. They had little money, and things were often tough. But they had never expected much. The 1920s had been really prosperous for one in three Canadians at most. The 1930s were prosperous for even fewer. Most of the others adapted to survive. It was difficult, often impossible, to do so with dignity and enjoyment if you lived on a dried-out farm in Saskatchewan or in an Atlantic fishing village, or if you were one of the many unemployed. To watch your soil being blown away, to grow crops or catch fish that no one would pay a decent price for, to apply again and again for menial jobs and yet fail to get one: that was to learn the meaning of despair. Many people had to live with that, with the reality or the fear of it. They found ways of escaping from it, at least temporarily, in churches, movies, sports, reading, or family life. It is impossible to believe, rosy memories notwithstanding, that they ever learned to like it.

REVIEW AND DISCUSSION

Key People and Ideas

Explain the importance of each of the following as they are discussed in the chapter.

W.A.C. Bennett	The Aird Commission
Charlie Millard	Old Age Pensions
Max Braithwaite	The Trades and Labour Congress
Foster Hewitt	The Congress of Industrial
Raymond Massey	Organizations
Dionne Quintuplets	The Social Service Council of Canada
Morley Callaghan	The CBC
Anne Marriott	Edmonton Commercial Graduates
Group of Seven	Maclean's
	Dominion Drama Festival

Analysing the Issues

Answer each of the following questions, which deal with important issues raised in the chapter.

1. What were the differences between the way of life of the wealthy, the middle class, the working class and the farmers during the 1930s?
2. What factors led to hostility towards immigrants to Canada during the 1930s?

Questions for Discussion

Think carefully about the following questions and discuss the issues they raise.

1. During the 1930s, the idea that governments should provide for old age pensions, health care, unemployment insurance and other forms of "social security" became accepted. Today, most Canadians consider these programmes to be a citizen's right. Do you think the situation in Canada during the 1930s justified the establishment of these programmes? Could Canadian governments afford them? Use specific evidence from the chapter to support your opinion.
2. Consider the possible recreational activities discussed in the latter part of this chapter. How do your opportunities for recreation today compare with what you might have done during the Depression? Explain your answer.

7

CANADA IN THE WORLD

The 1930s were years of war and rumours of war. Soon after the beginning of the decade Japan invaded Manchuria. The years that followed witnessed conflict in China, Ethiopia, Spain and many other places. In September 1939, Germany invaded Poland, setting off the second global war in a quarter century.

Canadian statesmen operated in the highly charged international environment of this period with a new degree of freedom. In the aftermath of the Great War, the British Empire began to turn into the British Commonwealth of Nations. The self-governing "white" Dominions gained autonomy in their relations with foreign countries.

Dominion Status and the Statute of Westminster

The process of redefining the status of the Dominions began during the 1914–18 war. The importance of the contribution that Canada, Australia, New Zealand and South Africa were making to the war effort gave them new weight and stature. Clearly they were no longer just dependencies of Great Britain. During the 1920s politicians and civil servants worked to bring the constitutional law into line with the new reality. In this task Canadians took an active but not a leading part. That fell to the governments of the Irish Free State, formed in the early 1920s, and South Africa. In these countries the desire for formal independence was stronger than in Canada, to say nothing of Australia and New Zealand. In the latter three countries the emotional ties that many people felt to Britain were still very strong.

An Imperial Conference in 1930 adopted a number of recommendations that were embodied in the Statute of Westminster. The British Parliament passed in in 1931. Soon afterwards the Parliament of Canada passed it also, but not until the agreement of the provinces had been secured.

The Statute of Westminster stated that any change in the royal title or succession required the assent of the Dominions. Thus in 1936 the Canadian and other Dominion governments were consulted about the formalities that surrounded the abdication of King Edward VIII and the succession of his brother, the Duke of York, who became King George VI.

The Statute also freed the Dominions from the provisions of the Colonial Laws Validity Act. This meant that they could henceforth repeal or alter any imperial law that was in force within their borders. No future imperial law would apply to a Dominion without its consent. Imperial restrictions on Dominion control over their merchant fleet disappeared. There was also clear recognition of the right of the Dominions to pass extra-territorial legislation, that is, laws having force beyond their own borders.

Not all imperial authority ended with the Statute of Westminster. In particular, the British Parliament was the only body

Opposite page:
King George VI and
Queen Elizabeth on their
Canadian tour, May
1939.

that could change or repeal the Statute itself. As well, the Statute denied power to the Parliament of Canada to amend the British North America Act. This was done at Canada's own request, after premiers L.-A. Taschereau of Quebec and Howard Ferguson of Ontario insisted on it. They wanted formal recognition that the BNA Act was a compact, or agreement, among the provinces of Canada; they did not want the federal government to have the power to change it unilaterally. The legal argument that underlay the provincial claim was not particularly strong. Nevertheless, in the interests of domestic peace, both Mackenzie King and R.B. Bennett accepted it. Of course, Canada could obtain the power to amend the BNA Act as soon as Canadian governments, federal and provincial, agreed on how to go about amending it. This they would not manage to do for another 50 years.

Agreement was finally reached in 1981, and is contained in the Constitution Act of 1982.

What exactly the Statute meant for Canada's relations with Great Britain was not entirely clear. Of key importance was the answer to the question: what would happen if Britain went to war? Would Canada be at war automatically, as in 1914? Or would she have the right to remain neutral, thus making a separate declaration of war necessary if she chose to side with Britain?

Experts gave conflicting answers to these questions. Some said that Canada's right to neutrality was secure; others said the opposite. Those who agreed that there was no right to neutrality when Britain went to war disagreed as to whether this was a good thing. Some of them were ardent imperialists who were prepared to stand by Britain come what may. Others were autonomists who believed the right to neutrality to be essential to national self-respect. Others again were isolationists who held that Canada had no real interest in possible British quarrels in Africa, Asia or even Europe. Many of these people, but by no means all, were French Canadians, and there were enough of them to influence Ottawa's foreign policy in the 1930s. This was true especially after 1935, when Mackenzie King returned to office. He enjoyed strong support in Quebec, where isolationist sentiment was dominant, and he intended to keep that support.

Edward VIII
Less than a year after he became king, Edward VIII abdicated. He wanted to marry an American divorcee, Mrs. Wallis Simpson. The Church of England, of which the monarch is the secular head, and the British government would not agree to this. The King, saying he could not live without the woman he loved, then left the throne to become the Duke of Windsor.

The Statute of Westminster conferred a new constitutional status on the Dominions. They were henceforth associated with the United Kingdom as equals within a free association, the British Commonwealth. Whatever this might mean in a time of crisis, Canada's relations with Britain and with the other Dominions were not yet foreign relations. When the Commonwealth countries met it was in a real way a family gathering.

Trade and Commerce

At the Imperial Conference of 1930, Prime Minister R.B. Bennett made a plea for a system of preferential tariffs within the British Empire. Each Empire country would give preference to the goods of other Empire countries over those from the non-British world. Bennett had no intention of reducing the protection enjoyed by Canadian-made goods in the Canadian market. The main Conservative slogan in the recent election campaign had been "Canada First." However, he hoped to make it easier for Canadian goods to compete with foreign ones in the United Kingdom market.

In 1930 this still ran counter to British policy. Since the late 1840s the British government had followed a policy of free trade, levying only low tariffs to provide the government with revenue. The British had not distinguished between Empire and non-Empire goods. Then the growing weakness of British industry during the early Depression years forced a change in trade policy. In 1931 Great Britain abandoned free trade.

This opened the way to trade negotiations involving the Empire as a whole. These took place in Ottawa in 1932. The talks were difficult; the tension was great. Nevertheless agreements were hammered out which gave Canada preferential access to the British market for a range of goods, raw, processed and manufactured. In turn many British and other Empire goods got increased preference from Canada. This was accomplished not through a lowering of Canadian tariffs on Empire goods, but through a further raising of tariffs on non-Empire goods, including those from the United States.

An increase in Canadian trade with Britain followed, offsetting to some extent the drop in exports to the United States that resulted from American tariff increases. Of course, Canadians continued to be eager to trade with the United States. Although the Bennett government met the higher American tariffs with higher tariffs of its own on American manufactured goods, the hope remained that trade barriers between Canada and the United States might be lowered.

At last, in 1934 the United States passed the Reciprocal Trade Agreements Act, which set the two countries on the road to freer trade. The Bennett government started discussions that led in 1935 to an agreement to reduce the level of many tariffs. By this time Mackenzie King was once again prime minister, however, and he got the political benefit of going to Washington to sign the treaty for Canada. Three years later King's government was able to negotiate a second, broader agreement. This signalled the beginning of an era of steadily growing trade with the United States.

North American Relations

A good deal of the nineteenth-century Canadian suspicion of Americans still lingered in the 1930s. Resentment against the Smoot–Hawley Tariff was strong. From his inauguration in March 1933, however, President Franklin Delano Roosevelt showed himself to be a good neighbour. He had many admirers in

Canada and he also had a personal tie with Canada: his summer home was on Campobello Island, just inside New Brunswick's border with Maine. Roosevelt favoured closer trade relations with Canada, and helped to clear the way to the trade agreements of 1935 and 1938. He also favoured the proposal for a St. Lawrence waterway. This would involve the construction of a seaway from the Gulf of St. Lawrence to Lake Superior, allowing ocean-going vessels to penetrate deep into the heart of the continent, as well as the construction of large hydro-electric generating facilities on the St. Lawrence River. The total cost was estimated at $500 million, a huge sum of money at that time. A treaty was signed in 1932, but there was considerable opposition to it. Seaports like Montreal and New York faced a loss of traffic. Hydro-electric power companies in New York State were hostile to the proposal as well, and many American legislators questioned its value. In the end the U.S. Senate failed to ratify the treaty.

Informal relations with the United States were closer in the 1930s than formal ones. Many years of migration between the two countries meant that hundreds of thousands of Canadians had relatives south of the border. In spite of the reduced incomes of the Depression years, there was a lot of tourism in both directions. There were those who worried about Canada's growing closeness to the United States. They usually pointed to popular culture as the area of greatest concern. Glossy magazines, radio, and the movies: these three, largely American in origin, were shaping the way Canadians saw the world.

No tradition of joint defence existed. Indeed, as late as the 1920s Canadian military strategists had a plan for a pre-emptive attack on the United States in the unlikely event that war might break out between that country and Great Britain. With war approaching in Europe in the later 1930s, however, an event took place that pointed to closer military co-operation between Canada and the United States. In 1938 President Roosevelt visited Kingston, Ontario, to receive an honorary degree from Queen's University. In the course of his convocation address he said: "The Dominion is part of the sisterhood of the British Empire. I give to you assurance that the people of the United States will not stand idly by if domination of Canadian soil is threatened by any other empire." What empire that might be he did not say, but presumably the threat would come from Japan or Germany.

Few Canadians in 1938 believed themselves to be in danger of attack. Prime Minister King told the House of Commons in that year: "The talk which one sometimes hears of aggressor nations planning to invade Canada and seize these tempting resources of ours is, to say the least, premature. It ignores our neighbours and our lack of neighbours." There was no threat from the United States and as yet, it seemed, no credible threat from any other

Government Income
The total income of the Canadian federal government in 1930 was $314 million.

country. The world was becoming more dangerous, however. There had been war between Japan and China for several years. In Europe the territorial ambitions of Germany and, to a lesser extent, Italy were a source of growing concern. Thus, although Canadians perceived no immediate threat, many of them found it reassuring that the American president was friendly.

The Ethiopian Crisis

Japan's attack on the Chinese province of Manchuria in 1931 excited little attention in Canada. The same was not true four years later when Italy, led by the fascist dictator Benito Mussolini, attacked the ancient kingdom of Ethiopia. Unlike the rest of Africa, Ethiopia had escaped conquest by a European power in the nineteenth century because it was mountainous and poor, and not considered worth the expense of conquering it. Mussolini's concern was not primarily economic, however. He wanted Italy to be greater among the nations of the earth, and an overseas empire seemed a necessary condition for this.

The Italian assault on Ethiopia began on October 4, 1935, creating a serious crisis for the League of Nations. The League had been formed after the Great War by the powers that had defeated the German and Austro–Hungarian empires. Although it was gravely weakened by the failure of the United States Senate to ratify American membership in it, the League nevertheless committed itself to protect member states against aggression. "Collective security" was the catch-word—but the League had no armed forces of its own. Any aggressor, therefore, had to be resisted by the member states. Many of these states did not believe in collective security strongly enough to oppose distant acts of aggression. Thus the Japanese conquest of Manchuria had proceeded unhindered, even though China, to which Manchuria belonged, was a member of the League. The Ethiopian crisis, therefore, was a second and crucially important test of the idea of collective security.

Article Ten of the League Convenant required that member states come to the aid of a member who was attacked. One potentially effective way was to impose economic sanctions against the aggressor. In the case of Italy this was a promising course of action. That country had no domestic sources of materials needed to fight a war: iron ore, nickel, rubber and petroleum. Faced with the threat of being denied these goods by League members, Italy might well end the aggression without member states themselves having had to go to war. If economic sanctions failed, League members could then consider military steps.

Canadian policy on this issue was unclear. Canada had insisted on joining the League of Nations as a sort of proof of the increased stature achieved during the Great War. This did not mean, however, that many Canadians believed in collective security. In fact, the Canadian government had steadfastly opposed the

Some 60 000 Canadians had died in northern France and Flanders in the 1914–18 conflict; these losses had brought about a desire to be isolated from future wars.

military side of Article Ten, the duty to resist aggression with military force if necessary. Canadian politicians knew, or thought they knew, that many Canadians were unwilling to become involved in an overseas war for a second time within 20 years.

In the early 1920s Canadian representatives had tried to modify Article Ten in such a way as to excuse smaller countries, like Canada, from having to participate in military action against an aggressor. To change the League Covenant required unanimous approval, and the Canadian attempt had failed. But it had come close enough to succeeding for most League members to realize that, even in a clear case of aggression, it would prove hard to get many members to agree to military action against the aggressor. Even economic sanctions might be difficult to impose.

When the Ethiopian crisis developed, R.B. Bennett's Conservatives were still in office in Ottawa. The 1935 election campaign was in full swing, however, distracting Prime Minister Bennett from foreign affairs. At first, therefore, he accepted the advice of the Undersecretary of State for External Affairs, Dr. O.D. Skelton, that Canada should not commit itself to any kind of sanctions until after the election. This decision appalled Canada's representatives at League headquarters in Geneva, Switzerland. Italy was clearly guilty of aggression, they argued early in October. Canada should be prepared to say so and to participate in economic sanctions.

On their advice Bennett overruled Skelton on October 10, and when the latter protested the prime minister said to him: "No one in Canada is going to deny Italy [is] guilty or object to our saying so. If they did, [I am] not going to wriggle out if it meant I didn't get one vote." Four days after he said this, his party suffered crushing defeat in the general election, though not, it is safe to say, because of Bennett's foreign policy. Five years of Depression had been enough to finish the Conservatives.

On October 23, 1935, Mackenzie King took office. He took a different view of sanctions. King believed, no doubt correctly, that many Canadians were sufficiently isolation-minded to reject the principle of collective security. He did not reject the idea of economic sanctions on principle, but he did fear taking bold steps that might raise the issue of Canadian participation in an overseas war. King knew that hostility in Quebec to such a war would be strong, and Quebec seats were an essential component in the recent Liberal election victory. It was therefore easy for King to persuade himself that war would threaten the unity of the Liberal party and the country.

During the transfer of power in Ottawa from the Conservatives to the Liberals, the senior Canadian diplomat in Geneva was Dr. W.A. Riddell. Ignoring Skelton's instructions to take no further position on proposals for sanctions, Riddell chose to follow an earlier directive that "any scheme of economic sanctions should be comprehensive." This led him in early November to propose that the League's embargo against Italy include "petroleum and derivatives; coal; iron, cast iron and steel." The sanctions steering committee, of which Canada was a member, quickly adopted the "Canadian proposal." Petroleum, of course, was the key product. If anything could force Italy to stop its invasion of Ethiopia, it was a petroleum embargo. This was doubly true because the American government, although not a member of the League, had indicated its willingness to put pressure on American oil companies to observe the embargo.

Riddell had taken a major step, but he had done so without Ottawa's authority. At first the Canadian government kept quiet in the hope that media attention would shift away from Riddell's action. When it did not, King decided that his government must repudiate Riddell's initiative before the League of Nations Assembly had an opportunity to discuss it. The repudiation came on December 2, 1935, in the form of a press statement by the acting Secretary of State for External Affairs, Ernest Lapointe. He was King's acknowledged Quebec lieutenant and the second most powerful man in the cabinet. Lapointe stated that Riddell's proposal "represented only his personal opinion . . . and not the

Providing medical aid for the Republicans during the Spanish Civil war, Dr. Norman Bethune created the world's first mobile blood transfusion service.

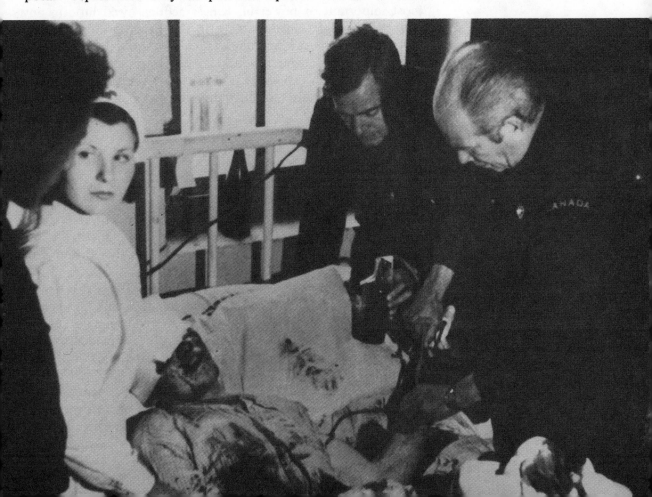

views of the Canadian government." When reporters questioned King about Lapointe's disclaimer he said: "After all, we are but 10 millions on the north end of a continent, and we should not strive to overplay our part." Bold initiatives were for other, more powerful countries.

The Italians defeated the Ethiopians and occupied their country while the League Assembly was still discussing the terms of an oil embargo. The incident did not show the League at its best. Indeed, with hindsight we know that the failure to deal effectively with the Ethiopian crisis signalled the end of the League of Nations as anything more than a forum for discussion. For the time being, collective security was dead. Mackenzie King did not yet see this and continued to fear that the principle of collective security might conceivably involve Canada in war. In 1936 he visited Geneva and told the League Assembly that henceforth it should rely solely on "conciliation, mediation, and the weight of world opinion" to prevent aggression and preserve peace. In any event, he continued, Canada would not accept "automatic commitments to the application of force."

Although Canada did its bit to pull whatever teeth the League of Nations had, it would be a mistake to attach much weight to its role. It was only one member state, and far from the most important or powerful. King's actions owed little to any consideration of Canada's place in the League, however, and much to what he saw as domestic realities. Few Canadians had any use for the League beyond its value in enhancing Canada's status as a country. The League of Nations Society in Canada was small; internationalists were few in number.

The Spanish Civil War

In the spring of 1936 a war broke out in Spain. Conservatives and fascists, as well as much of the army, led by General Francisco Franco, rose up against the Spanish Republic. The only country to come to the aid of the left-leaning Republican government was Soviet Russia. Both fascist Italy and Nazi Germany offered the insurgents material support and trained manpower. Internally divided on the merits of the struggle, countries like Britain and France remained officially neutral.

For three years the war raged ferociously. It agitated people around the world, including Canadians. Quebec opinion strongly favoured the insurgents, who were supported by much of the Spanish Roman Catholic Church. Some other Canadians, however, saw the insurgents simply as fascists, proxies for Hitler and Mussolini. Such Canadians supported the work of Dr. Norman Bethune and his Canadian Blood Transfusion Service in Spain, and some of them volunteered for the International Brigades trying to help the Republic. Eventually the Mackenzie–Papineau

The Spanish republican government was anti-clerical, seeking to secularize education and other important social services, and to reduce the wealth of the Roman Catholic Church. This made conflict with the bishops inevitable.

Battalion, named after the leaders of the 1837 uprisings in Upper and Lower Canada, was formed. Approximately 1240 brave young Canadians served in Spain; almost a third of them died there. After Spain herself and France, Canada made the highest per capita manpower contribution to the Republican cause.

The Canadian government did not approve of Canadians fighting in Spain. In 1937 it passed the Foreign Enlistment Act which, among other things, made it an offence to enlist in the armed forces of a foreign state like Spain. The act was a concession to Quebec opinion. By staying officially neutral, however, the Canadian government gave equal moral standing to the insurgents and to the forces defending the Republic. Critics saw this as part and parcel of the western democracies' shilly-shallying attitude to fascism.

Canada, Great Britain and Appeasement

From 1936 on the League of Nations was no longer an important feature in Canadian foreign policy. The British connection loomed all the larger as a result. If Britain went to war, would Canada follow? King's promise that in such an event "Parliament will decide" satisfied neither those who believed that Canada should stand by Britain automatically, nor those who wanted the country to stay out of a "British war." One of the latter, constitutional lawyer Frank R. Scott, asked impatiently in 1937: "What will Parliament decide? To back out of a war in which [Canada] is already committed on the side of Great Britain? Or merely how many troops to send? It is at present constitutionally impossible for Parliament to decide to remain neutral in a British war."

The person to whom Scott was writing was J.S. Woodsworth, leader of the national CCF. Woodsworth tried to pin the prime minister down in the House of Commons. King, prudent and wily, foiled all such attempts. He worried little about the constitutional point that bothered Scott and Woodsworth. His concern was to take a united Canada into war should conflict prove unavoidable. He did not believe that public discussion, or a clarification of Canada's constitutional rights, would make his task easier. On the contrary, he feared that discussion or the process of clarification would divide both the country and his party. He therefore avoided it.

Personally King hated and feared war. Moreover, the country was totally unready for war. In the early 1930s the armed forces had been a favourite target for budget cuts. During the Bennett years military spending sank to its lowest point in over two decades, little more than $13 million in 1933-34. In 1933 the Chief of the General Staff, General A.G.L. McNaughton, almost sacrificed the Royal Canadian Navy altogether in order to be able to maintain a minimal air force. The permanent forces dropped to below 7000, and, as McNaughton pointed out in April 1935, they had almost no equipment or ammunition. This state of affairs, he wrote, "can be viewed only with the gravest concern. And with the rapidly deteriorating international situation the position is becoming more and more disquieting." Every branch of the services was suffering from gross neglect.

In itself that did not trouble King greatly. He believed that Canadians and, indeed, the British, desired peace, not war. All the same, if Britain did go to war, it seemed likely that her reasons would satisfy most English Canadians. French Canadians would be more sceptical, however, and they would resist if participation in a British war was seen to be taken for granted. Prudence demanded that King claim freedom of action for Parliament—while at the same time increasing arms expenditures, just in case. Small wonder that he avoided detailed discussion of foreign policy. In his view it could only be harmful to national unity. Besides, it might be quite unnecessary: war in Europe might be avoided.

From 1936 into 1939, Mackenzie King—and with him most Canadians—supported the British and French policy of appeasement. The leaders of both Britain and France clung to the belief that if the "reasonable demands" of Adolf Hitler could be met, war need not come about. Many felt that Germany should be freed from punitive and humiliating features of the Treaty of Versailles so long as this did not involve the restoration of territory taken from Germany as a result of that treaty. Thus Nazi Germany was able to rearm well beyond the low levels permitted by the treaty. In 1936 France did not intervene when German troops entered the Rhineland, an area of Germany that the treaty had made a demilitarized zone. Two years later the European powers looked the other way when the Germans annexed Austria.

Appeasement had critics in the 1930s, and it has had virtually nothing but critics since. The policy was widely popular at the time, however, and for good reason. Memories of the extraordinarily destructive 1914–18 war were still strong; no reasonable person wanted another one. There was a sense that the Treaty of Versailles had punished Germany too heavily. Beyond that, Hitler's demands did not affect any vital British or French interests, or so it seemed. Some western statesmen hoped that by indulging Germany they might encourage her to turn eastward and attack the Soviet Union in a war that would exhaust both countries. Many people were as hostile to the Soviets as they were to the Nazis, and the prospect of such a war was not unpleasing to them.

King fervently hoped that Germany and Britain would not come to blows. Should they do so, he knew, Canada's entry into the war could not be averted. It would be much better if the occasion did not arise at all. Given this frame of mind, King was predisposed to an optimistic assessment of Hitler's aims.

The two men met in Berlin, the German capital, in 1937. King told Hitler that in case of a war of aggression against Britain, "nothing in the world would keep the Canadian people from being at the side of Britain." He then allowed the German dictator, who could be charming, to lull him into a pleasant sense of security. King later told a newspaper reporter that he found Hitler to be "a simple sort of peasant, not very intelligent and no serious danger to anyone," whose territorial aims were limited to neighbouring regions that contained large German-speaking populations. As a result, King "looked for no early trouble in Europe."

Hitler probably did not want war, certainly not with Britain and France. He was quite prepared to risk it, however, in order to achieve his goals. In the summer of 1938 he made a claim to the Sudetenland, an area of Czechoslovakia along the German border where many German-speaking people lived. The Czech government was ready to resist the German land grab, but it needed the support of the two countries, France and Britain, that had guaranteed its border with Germany. Faced with the real possibility of having to go to war, these two countries caved in. At a conference in Munich, Germany, in September of 1938, Britain, France, Italy and Germany reached agreement on the transfer of the Sudetenland to Germany. The Czechs were simply instructed to give up their territory. For his part, Hitler said that he had no more territorial claims in Europe.

The Canadian prime minister, W.L. Mackenzie King, visits Berlin in 1937.

The Canadian government had supported the conciliatory stand taken by the British prime minister, Neville Chamberlain. Like Chamberlain, Mackenzie King hoped that the agreement at Munich would mean "peace in our time." Again like Chamberlain, he was nonetheless taking steps to prepare for the possibility of war. In doing so, however, he was careful to maintain the appearance of autonomy. In 1938, Britain asked if it could train pilots in Canada for the Royal Air Force (RAF). If Canada agreed, would it not automatically be at war if Britain went to war? The Canadian government refused.

Unwillingness to be seen to commit Canada in advance to a possible war explains two years of indecision over a contract for the manufacture of Bren guns for the British Army. Ottawa hesitated from 1936 until 1938 before finally suggesting a manufacturer to the British government. Canadian rearmament, also a touchy issue, proceeded somewhat more quickly. The government raised the defence estimates for 1936–37 to $24 million, and for 1937–38 to $35 million. Since the main justification for these increases was the need to defend Canada's coastal waters, the Navy and the Air Force were the prime beneficiaries. Even so, there was vigorous criticism of the increased spending. In Parliament a CCF member, Grant MacNeil, argued that there was no direct threat to Canadian shores.

Experts in the Department of National Defence disagreed. They stated in September 1936 that there were potential threats both by air and by sea, threats against which Canada was quite defenceless. An enemy could seize territory in the Arctic and construct bases for use by hostile bomber planes and submarines.

Although the King government accepted the view of the experts, the additions it made to the defence budget were only half of what the military leaders had asked for. Furthermore, the government froze the defence estimates at $35 million for 1938–39, the last prewar year. King was little concerned about CCF criticism. What did matter to him was that a good many French-Canadian members of his own parliamentary caucus opposed further increases in defence spending.

The Coming of War

There was a serious turn for the worse in European affairs in March 1939. Hitler broke the promise he had made the previous autumn to respect Czechoslovakia's new borders. German troops occupied the western part of the country, including the capital, Prague. The eastern part became a German puppet state, Slovakia. Greatly disillusioned by Hitler's actions, Neville Chamberlain and his cabinet set British policy on a new course. They abandoned appeasement. Germany was now claiming some of the territories it had lost to Poland in 1919. Britain joined France in offering Poland a guarantee of help in case of German aggression.

By now King was manoeuvering to line up a united Canada behind Britain should it come to war between Britain and Germany. In order to reassure French-Canadian opinion, King pledged in the House of Commons on March 30, 1939, that in case of war there would be no conscription for overseas military service. (The new leader of the Conservative Party, Dr. R.J. Manion, had already made the same pledge.) A long visit to Canada by King George VI and his wife, Queen Elizabeth, in the early summer of 1939 heightened interest in the British connection.

In Europe the efforts of Britain and France shifted to an attempt to show Germany that an attack on Poland was not in her own interest. To this end it was necessary to forge an alliance that offered some prospect of being able to resist a German attack on Poland. For this the co-operation of the Soviets was essential. Neither the Poles nor the Soviets were eager to co-operate, however. During the Polish–Soviet War of the early 1920s Poland had conquered a lot of land from Russia. The Soviet dictator, Josef Stalin, suddenly saw an opportunity to regain this land while avoiding the war with Germany that he feared. In spite of mutual suspicion and hostility, Nazi Germany and Soviet Russia signed a non-aggression pact on August 23, 1939. Attached to it was a secret document in which the two countries approved each other's territorial claims in eastern Europe.

The stage was set for war. No longer fearing Russian intervention, and convinced that Britain and France would find a way of backing out of their commitments to Poland, Hitler made his move. On September 1, 1939, in the early hours of the morning, Germany invaded Poland.

Hitler, knowing that neither Britain nor France could give effective aid to Poland, gambled that their governments would not go to war. He lost. The two western powers issued an ultimatum: either Germany withdrew from Poland by September 3, or they would declare war on Germany. Hitler ignored these threats. At 11:00 A.M. on September 3, Britain declared war. France followed six hours later.

> Early in the morning of the day that Britain entered the war I walked along Sparks Street towards my office in the East Block. As it was Sunday, all the shops were closed, and a strange silence—a silence one could almost feel—seemed to brood over and enfold the entire city. The few people I met were depressed, grim, and monosyllabic. When they spoke it was in anger and revulsion. Memories of 1914–18 were in everyone's mind, and we were now convinced that it was all going to happen again.

Thus Dr. Hugh Keenleyside, then working in the Department of External Affairs in Ottawa, remembers September 3, 1939. He recalls that there was also a certain sense of relief. The uncertainty was over. War had threatened for years; it had arrived at last and

Canadian Declaration of
War
Vincent Massey, the
Canadian High
Commissioner to Britain,
wrote: "It was our
Government's intention to
issue the proclamation at
one o'clock Ottawa time
on the assembly of
Parliament. The date of
the proclamation was to be
September 10, one week
after the declaration of
war by Britain. The
difference in dates was
largely due to a desire to
indicate Canada's national
independence. In effect, of
course, we were at war as
soon as Great Britain, all
war measures being in full
operation."

people would have to cope with it. However, there was no enthusiasm as there had been 25 years before.

The cabinet decided to call Parliament into special session on September 8. From the third, however, the government had been behaving as if the country were already at war. There were Canadians who objected to this; some of them thought Canada should remain neutral. One was J.S. Woodsworth. For many years a pacifist, he resigned as leader of the CCF when most of the party's national council decided, although many of them reluctantly, to support Canada's entry into the war. Another was Dr. O.D. Skelton, the Undersecretary of State for External Affairs, who told King that he did not think Britain's moral case was compelling enough to justify Canadian participation. There were others, in English and especially French Canada, who opposed going to war. They were a minority, however. Most Canadians were ready to line up behind Britain. They were not enthusiastic, but they were ready.

On September 10, 1939, Canada declared war on Germany. This was a formality, confirming what everybody had already assumed to be the case. Young men had begun lining up at armed forces recruiting centres throughout Canada more than a week before. The War Measures Act had been proclaimed on September 1; the Defence of Canada regulations had come into effect on September 3.

The war was one that few Canadians wanted. Yet it offered at least the welcome prospect of change. Unemployment and low prices for farm products did not disappear overnight. In the public consciousness, however, the war was now the dominant reality. The Depression became a memory.

King's skilful manoeuvering had paid off, moreover. Canada was very nearly united in entering the war. At the beginning recruitment was almost as good in Quebec as in the rest of the country. There was another indication that French-speaking Quebec was not strongly opposed, as some commentators in the 1930s had assumed it would be. Premier Maurice Duplessis called an election in the early fall of 1939. He objected to the growth in Ottawa's powers as a result of the War Measures Act, and called on the voters of Quebec to support him. This turned out to be a mistake. The federal cabinet ministers from Quebec, led by the Minister of Justice, Ernest Lapointe, entered the campaign. They threatened to resign their cabinet positions should Duplessis' *Union nationale* be re-elected. Their presence in Mackenzie King's government, they pointed out, was Quebec's best guarantee against conscription for overseas military service. The Quebec voters, some of them upset with Duplessis for his failure to live up to his 1936 election promises, others fearing the loss of effective cabinet representation in Ottawa, dealt Duplessis a crushing defeat. Led by

Adélard Godbout, the provincial Liberals returned to office.

Neither Canada's entry into the war nor the outcome of the Quebec election meant that French or English Canadians had come to recognize fully their place in an interdependent world. They did not go to war because of internationalist ideals, or because they strongly supported Poland. By and large they went to war from a sense of filial duty, because Britain went to war. Even though it was a formality, however, the separate declaration of war on September 10, 1939, was important. It marked the beginning of real Canadian independence. Furthermore, the Second World War would teach Canadians what, in spite of the 1914–18 war and the Depression, they had not yet learned: actions in seemingly remote places could affect Canada very much.

The war, finally, did end the Depression. A young man in Anne Marriott's poem "The Wind Our Enemy" says: "Maybe there'll be a war and we'll get paid to fight." There *was* a war, and they *were* paid to fight. Soon the economy, stimulated by government spending on the war effort, started growing dramatically. When people who lived through the 1930s are asked: "What ended the Depression?" they quite properly answer: "The war."

REVIEW AND DISCUSSION

Key People and Ideas
Explain the importance of each of the following as they are discussed in the chapter.

Franklin Delano Roosevelt	The Statute of Westminster
Dr. W.A. Riddell	Ethiopian Crisis
Adolf Hitler	The League of Nations
Neville Chamberlain	Mackenzie–Papineau Battalion

Analysing the Issues
Answer each of the following questions, which deal with important issues raised in the chapter.

1. What evidence was there during the 1930s of improving relations between Canada and the United States?
2. What factors led Mackenzie King to reject the idea of "collective security"?
3. What political factors led Mackenzie King to announce that should Britain go to war, "Parliament will decide" the issue of Canadian participation?

Question for Discussion
Think carefully about the following question and discuss the issues it raises.

1. During the 1930s, the leaders of western governments chose to seek peace with Adolf Hitler by appeasement. Do you think a different course might have avoided the Second World War?

EPILOGUE: A LONG SHADOW

The 1930s were years of great economic distress and suffering. They were also years of conflict, as social groups fought for their share of a shrinking national income, as municipalities quarreled with provincial governments and provinces with Ottawa over revenues and programmes, and as countries contended with each other over markets, resources and territory. The spectre of a renewed world war came nearer as the decade wore on. For many Canadians the Depression years were years of despair. They despaired of good times ever coming again, or of nations and peoples being able to avoid a war that threatened to be at least as destructive as the 1914–18 war.

It may seem surprising, but these years of misery and conflict produced little structural change in Canada. At the outbreak of war in 1939, the country's economic, social and political structures were much as they had been at the time of the crash ten years before. Political parties old and new had made many proposals for change, but most Canadians stuck to well-worn paths. The serious problems that confronted them did not prompt new kinds of thought or action. Rather, they reinforced habits of caution.

The Depression's Long-Range Influence

Even if there was little real change in the 1930s, the Depression cast a long shadow. During the Second World War, with the economy running at full capacity, Canadians began to worry that the end of the war would bring renewed unemployment when those who were serving in the armed forces returned to civilian life and war production came to an end. "There were misgivings and fears," C.D. Howe, the wartime Minister of Munitions and Supply, recalled later. "Memories of the depressed thirties were in everyone's mind."

Planning for postwar Canada began early. In 1941 the federal government formed a Committee on Reconstruction. One major result was the *Report on Social Security for Canada,* prepared by Leonard Marsh and issued in 1943. The following year Ottawa established three new departments: Reconstruction, National Health and Welfare, and Veterans' Affairs. The Speech from the Throne on January 27, 1944, stated that the "post-war object of our domestic policy is social security and human welfare." The government also pledged itself to guarantee "useful employment for all who are willing to work." In April 1945, the government's "White Paper on Employment and Income" asserted that "the maintenance of a high and stable level of employment and income is a major aim of government policy.''

The Liberals' new commitment to high employment and social security owed a lot to the fear of a revived Depression. It also owed something to their recognition of a political threat from the left. For two years after 1941, the CCF steadily gained support. In 1943 the party won 34 seats in an Ontario election and became the Opposition. By September 1943, a nation-wide Gallup poll disclosed that 29 percent of the electorate supported the CCF. The Liberal and Conservative parties each had the support of 28 percent. The CCF was particularly strong in the West, and in 1944 formed the provincial government in Saskatchewan.

The CCF's new-found strength fed on widespread fears of post-war depression, but also on a growing belief that Canadians were entitled to higher standards of health and welfare than they had enjoyed before the war. People were making sacrifices during the war; they looked for some form of compensation. It is not altogether surprising that the CCF's support was strongest in the armed forces.

Whatever the sources of the challenge from the left, the Mackenzie King government responded to it. It did not limit itself to promises: the introduction in 1944 of family allowances, which had been a key recommendation in the Marsh Report of 1943, was an important step towards the welfare state. So was the 1945 White Paper and the accompanying "Green Book," which contained the proposals whereby the federal government hoped to finance its new schemes.

The Liberal initiatives set the country on a new course. They helped to re-elect the party in 1945, and although the party's reformist impulse weakened after the election, it did not vanish completely. During the quarter century that followed, Ottawa gradually and haltingly expanded the welfare state, and provincial governments took important steps in the same direction. Most significant was the conviction that the mass unemployment Canadians had suffered in the 1930s must not be allowed to happen again. Making sure it did not became one of the objectives of Ottawa's management of the economy. The provinces shared this objective, which was perhaps the key legacy of the 1930s.

There were others. The Depression caused physical and psychological damage, the effects of which are hard to assess. Who can tell what price in personal health, physical and emotional, the children of the 1930s paid and are paying for their deprivation during those years? Then there are the lessons that Canadians drew from the Depression experience. Many people became aware that the independence and security they derived from work were largely illusory. Their incomes, whether they worked on the farm or on the ocean, in mines, forests, factories, stores or offices, on

The Welfare State
The welfare state is committed to "the broad goals of economic development, full employment, equality of opportunity for the young, social security, and protected minimum standards as regards not only income, but nutrition, housing, health, and education for all people of all regions and social groups." (Gunnar Myrdal)

trains or on construction sites, were at the mercy of economic forces that they could not control. The loss of income brought with it a loss of status and even ultimately a loss of self-respect. All this fed a disturbing sense of insecurity. Everything they had could be lost again.

Working-class Canadians had considerable experience of unemployment and loss of income before the 1930s. That was generally less true of middle-class people. Everyone who had to ask for relief felt the stigma, the disgrace, but those who were least used to unemployment probably felt it most deeply of all. Moreover, the fear of it affected many who did not themselves lose their jobs. The fear persisted long after the Depression ended, and ensured continued middle-class support for government policies that promoted full employment.

That support continued into the 1970s. Since then it has weakened. Those Canadians who have vivid memories of the Depression and its hardships are now in their late fifties or older. Their influence on government policy-making is waning, except in the area of pensions. Canadian memories of the 1930s have dimmed. Most working Canadians, to say nothing of their school-age children, are familiar with the features of the welfare state while scarcely knowing what preceded it. As a consequence they have come to take the welfare state for granted and to be increasingly critical of it.

In the 1980s Canada has higher levels of unemployment than it has had since the 1930s. Ottawa and the provinces seem unwilling or unable to pursue policies of full employment any longer. Faced with the falling revenues that always accompany economic downturns, governments are pursuing restraint. They seem loath to devise effective employment-creating programmes for fear these will cost too much. We hear of cutbacks everywhere. Policies that proved themselves to be inadequate in the 1930s are presented as new wisdom 50 years later. If they failed to put people back to work in the Depression years and to make them better off, can they succeed now? There is no agreement about the answer to this question. In many ways Canadian circumstances differ from those in the 1930s; in other ways they are very similar. We do know, however, that millions of Canadians continue to live in poverty, insecurity and fear. For many people the 1980s, like the 1930s, are years of despair.

Further Reading

- Braithwaite, Max. *The Hungry Thirties.* Toronto: McClelland and Stewart, 1977. A lively and profusely illustrated social history of the decade.
- Broadfoot, Barry. *Ten Lost Years.* Toronto: Doubleday, 1973. Although this collection of interviews with people who lived through the Depression needs to be used with caution—people's memories are defective—it offers many fascinating insights into the lives of ordinary people during the 1930s.
- Cook, Ramsay, comp. *The Politics of Discontent.* Toronto: University of Toronto Press, 1967. This book contains four articles on provincial and national protest parties in the 1930s, including studies of William Aberhart, T.D. Pattullo and H.H. Stevens.
- Dumas, Evelyn. *The Bitter Thirties in Quebec.* Montreal: Black Rose Books, 1975. This study deals primarily with labour unrest in Quebec during the Depression.
- Eayrs, James. *In Defence of Canada,* vol. 2. Toronto: University of Toronto Press, 1965. This is a study of Canadian defence policies during the years 1935 through 1939. Though intended for a scholarly audience, it is well written and quite accessible.
- Gray, James. *Men Against the Desert.* Saskatoon: Western Producer Prairie Books, 1965. This is a very readable account of the Prairie Farm Rehabilitation Act and its background.
  ————. *The Winter Years.* Toronto: Macmillan, 1966. With this book Gray, a well-known journalist, has provided an excellent first-person account of the Depression on the Canadian prairies.
- Grayson, L.M. and Bliss, Michael, eds. *The Wretched of Canada.* Toronto: University of Toronto Press, 1971. This is an affecting selection of letters written by poor Canadians to Prime Minister R.B. Bennett during the years 1930–35.
- Horn, Michiel, ed. *The Dirty Thirties.* Toronto: Copp Clark, 1972. This is a useful collection of documents and articles covering all aspects of life in Canada during the Depression.
- Howard, Victor. *"We Were the Salt of the Earth!"* Regina: Canadian Plains, 1985. A narrative account of the On-To-Ottawa Trek and Regina Riot in 1935, this book makes skilful use of both interviews and documents.
- Hutcheson, Sydney. *Depression Stories.* Vancouver: New Star, 1976. This is a down-to-earth volume of reminiscences by a man who looked for work all over southern British Columbia during the 1930s and sometimes managed to find it.
- Livesay, Dorothy. *Right Hand, Left Hand.* Erin, Ont.: Press Porcépic, 1977. A memoir by a poet and political activist, this book gives excellent insight into the problems of women during the Depression.
- Neatby, H. Blair. *The Politics of Chaos.* Toronto: Macmillan, 1972. A brief and interesting introduction to the politics of the Depression years.
- Thompson, John Herd, with Seager, Allen. *Canada 1922–1939.* Toronto: McClelland and Stewart, 1985. Part of the Canadian Centenary Series, this contains the best survey of Canadian history in the 1930s.
- Wilbur, J.R.H. *The Bennett Administration.* Ottawa: Canadian Historical Association, 1969. This booklet give a brief overview of the government of R.B. Bennett. Unfortunately no good biography of Bennett is available.

Index

Page numbers in italics refer to illustrations, captions and/or margin notes.